"In business and in life, controlling one's own destiny is everything. And in today's ever-changing world of college sports, the new NIL rules present previously unimaginable potential for student athletes to do just that. But with the power and potential of NIL also comes great responsibility and plenty of pitfalls. So now's the time to get your head in the game, and this book, *Unlocking the Power of NIL*, is a great first step."

—**GUY FIERI**, celebrity chef and television personality

"As someone deeply invested in the development and success of student athletes, I highly recommend *Unlocking the Power of NIL*. This book provides invaluable insights and practical guidance that will empower young athletes to navigate their journeys both on and off the field. Jason Grilli's team and expertise and passion shine through every page, making it a must-read for anyone serious about excelling in the NIL space."

—**JIM CAVALE**, Athletes.org Founder and Chairman and three-time Inc. 5000 Entrepreneur

"NIL has changed the game for collegiate athletes, leveling the playing field and opening doors that were once firmly closed. *Unlocking the Power of NIL* is a must-read for any athlete looking to harness these new opportunities responsibly and effectively. With insightful strategies and real-world advice, this book provides the tools necessary to build a lasting legacy, both in sports and beyond."

—**GARY SHEFFIELD**, former MLB All-Star and World Series Champion

"As a college athlete from the pre-NIL era, I can't imagine how difficult it must be for today's student athletes to navigate this new world. This book shares valuable guidance and information that will help them make the best decisions for themselves so they can be as successful as possible both on and off the field."

—**LINDSAY BERRA**, sports journalist

UNLOCKING
THE
POWER
OF NIL

THE KEYS TO MONETIZING
YOUR ATHLETIC POTENTIAL

JASON GRILLI

KEYSTONE NIL PUBLISHING

UNLOCKING THE POWER OF NIL
The Keys to Monetizing Your Athletic Potential
First Edition

ISBN 978-1-5445-4632-2 *Hardcover*
   978-1-5445-4631-5 *Paperback*
   978-1-5445-4633-9 *Ebook*
   978-1-5445-4634-6 *Audiobook*

This book is dedicated to my mom and dad, my "Creation Team," who nurtured me from the ground up and instilled in me the values and determination that have guided me throughout my life. You both have been the architects of my character and my pillars of support in every endeavor. Your lessons have always reminded me of a truth beautifully encapsulated by Baseballism: "The name on the front of the jersey represents who you play for; the name on the back of the jersey represents who raised you. Do them both justice." This book is a testament to how deeply those words resonate with me. Thank you for everything.

—Jason Grilli

CONTENTS

FOREWORD

*by Tony Clark , Executive Director of
the Major League Baseball Players Association*

"It was the best of times, it was the worst of times," is a famous line from Charles Dickens' book, *A Tale of Two Cities*. It is perhaps the most illustrative way to describe the challenges and opportunities we face as a sports community in the new amateur Name, Image, and Likeness landscape.

As a former college basketball player, Major League Baseball Player, and father of three children who are former and current college athletes, my experience in athletics runs the gamut. One truth remains when it comes to player advocacy—some are in it for the right reasons, but some are not. The latter group will often disguise itself as trying to help athletes, but their true motivations eventually become apparent when money comes into the picture.

This is why players' associations and unions are considered a trusted source of support and information. Their motivations are simple and fundamental: to protect and advance the rights and interests of their members. Those who have been members of a players' association and pro athletes like Jason Grilli are best equipped to address deeper issues for the next generation of athletes. Moreover, they do so with no other motivation than to help.

Unlocking the Power of NIL is a resource for athletes at all levels and is devoid of the politics and personal interests that seem to permeate every facet of the NIL conversation. This Playbook offers a roadmap for athletes and their parents to follow. It also answers questions that many people have but may be uncomfortable asking.

Taking it a step further, it is dangerous and often expensive to either not ask the right questions or trust that the person that the athlete does ask has the right answers. Dangerous in that the wrong answer can actually damage the athlete and his or her reputation. It can be expensive because the opportunities lost due to bad advice can lead to a lessening of the athlete's earning potential away from the court or the field. To be certain, even as a professional athlete, their earning potential is relatively short—even if that athlete has a long professional career. As a result, it is paramount to be in a position to maximize their opportunities for whatever window of time they might have as an athlete. *Unlocking the Power of NIL* gives them the best chance to make the right decisions in the short window they have as an athlete.

As a former athlete, and now as a sports executive, I know there is one fundamental truism: Educated Athletes make Educated Decisions. Balancing their responsibilities as a student *and* as an athlete necessitates that they equip themselves to navigate both strategically and purposefully. As Benjamin Franklin famously said, "By failing to prepare, you are preparing to fail." This could not be more true in the area of NIL and its ever-changing landscape.

Whether you are an athlete or an athlete advocate, for your well-being, take the time to educate yourself about NIL. The two most commonly asked questions about NIL are; "How do I prepare and protect myself?" and, "How do I put myself in the best position to make good decisions in this brave new world of NIL?"

Unlocking the Power of NIL should be your first step in that journey!

A NOTE FROM JASON

Ladies and gentlemen,

Reflecting on a collective journey in professional sports, I am drawn to an often overlooked yet pivotal aspect of pursuing sports excellence: protecting one's Name Image and Likeness. I had the privilege of playing Major League Baseball for nearly two decades. Today, my team and I share the wisdom gained throughout my career, highlighting the ever-increasing importance of safeguarding these valuable assets, especially for amateur student athletes aspiring to reach professional levels.

In sports, the focus is often on the athlete's time with their jersey on, encompassing years of training, competing, and striving for greatness. However, there comes a time when the jersey must come off, whether by choice or circumstance. This transition, faced by every athlete, can be one of the most challenging and defining moments. Protecting one's Name, Image, and Likeness becomes paramount in this phase.

In the grand scheme of life, an athlete's career is remarkably short-lived. The crowd's roar and teammates' camaraderie shape us, but they are finite experiences. As we step into the next chapter of our lives, we must leverage the goodwill, connections, and reputation built throughout our athletic careers. Our Name, Image, and Likeness emerge as our most valuable assets here.

In the following pages, we will delve into this subject, drawing from our collective experiences and observations to illuminate why safeguarding your Name, Image, and Likeness is not just a matter of choice but a necessity. We will explore the benefits of wise decisions and the potential pitfalls of neglect and offer practical advice for student athletes on protecting their brand and laying the foundation for a successful professional transition.

Our goal is to inspire and empower the next generation of student athletes to pursue their dreams with passion and dedication, armed with knowledge and understanding to protect their reputations. The world of sports is a remarkable journey, and we wish for every aspiring athlete to experience it fully, both on and off the field.

As we explore the importance of safeguarding your Name, Image, and Likeness, we invite you to reflect on your aspirations and consider the lessons we've learned. Let us recognize that in the world of sports, your name is more than just a label; it's a legacy in the making.

With gratitude and anticipation,
Jason Grilli, a.k.a. "GrillCheese"

INTRODUCTION

As you flip open the pages of this book, consider it an invitation—an invitation to step onto a field that is as exciting, challenging, and rewarding as any athletic competition you've experienced. It's a field where the strengths, agility, and focus you've developed as an athlete will continue to serve you well. The difference? Instead of a ball, puck, or racket, the tools of this game are negotiation, marketing, and entrepreneurship. Welcome to the arena of monetizing your NIL.

As a student athlete, you have been graced with a unique position in society. You're admired and recognized, and your story inspires many. You've mastered discipline and dedication, pushed through the pain of practice, and celebrated the joy of victory. Now, with recent changes in the world of collegiate athletics, you have an extraordinary opportunity to tap into the power of your NIL to build a platform for yourself beyond your sport.

The NIL ruling has made it possible for you to benefit economically from your brand while still in school, and it's a game-changer, but it comes with its own set of challenges. Legal complexities, contractual obligations, and financial considerations come into play. How do you navigate these to come out on top? How do you transition your sporting success into the entrepreneurial realm without losing yourself in the process?

Unlocking the Power of NIL is your guidebook for this journey. This book does not merely seek to teach you the basics of leveraging your NIL, but also to prepare you for the real world—a world where financial acumen and legal competency are paramount. It aims to provide you with the knowledge and tools needed to successfully navigate this new landscape while adhering to NCAA rules and regulations.

Within these pages, you will find insights from top legal experts, successful entrepreneurs, and athletes who have navigated the path you're on. You'll learn about personal branding, contract negotiation, money management, entrepreneurship, and much more. It's designed to equip you with the tools needed to not only understand the opportunities that NIL brings but also to seize them effectively.

We believe that your athletic journey has prepared you for this moment. The same skills that allow you to excel in sports—discipline, resilience, and strategic thinking—are exactly what you need to thrive in the world of business. We are here to show you how.

This book is not just about monetizing your NIL. It's about unleashing your potential, building a lasting legacy, and making the most out of your hard-earned recognition. We hope that as you turn the pages, you'll feel empowered to take control of your future, transition seamlessly from an athlete to an entrepreneur, and leverage your NIL for success that extends far beyond the game.

Are you ready to unlock the power of your Name, Image, and Likeness? If your answer is a resounding yes, then let the journey begin.

ONE

THE BASICS OF NIL

"You will be out of your jersey longer than you will be in it! I urge students and professional athletes to cherish their time in athletic jerseys, symbolic of our innate drive, and talents. It's crucial to establish a platform that honors and preserves your legacy and name beyond the athletic journey, which is fleeting."
—JASON GRILLI, A.K.A. "GRILLCHEESE"

U nderstanding NIL is pivotal in appreciating the evolving landscape of collegiate athletics and its intersection with entrepreneurship. As a student athlete, your NIL refers to your personal brand. Your **N**ame represents who you are, your **I**mage reflects how you appear to others, and your **L**ikeness encapsulates the unique attributes that distinguish you from others. Together they form your identity, and it is this identity that the recent changes in legislation now allow you to monetize while you're still in school.

Your *Name* is your moniker, the label that others recognize you by. It's your first point of identification and an essential component of your brand. Whether it's the name you were given at birth or a nickname you've adopted along your journey, your name is the vehicle through which you build a reputation.

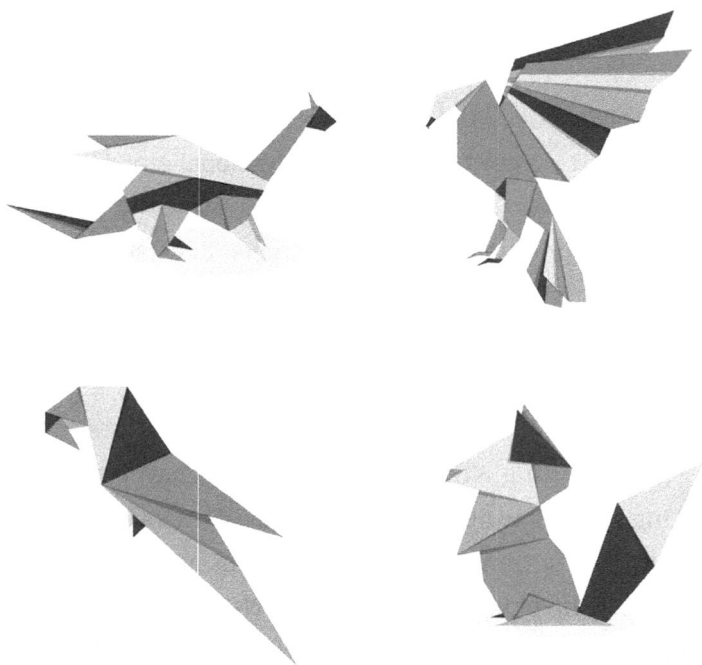

Your *Image*, on the other hand, is your visual representation. It's how people see you and includes photographs, video footage, and other visual depictions. Your image is the face of your brand; it's what people recognize, remember, and associate with your name.

Lastly, your *Likeness* refers to the unique characteristics that set you apart, including your voice, signature, gestures, and other distinctive traits. In essence, your likeness is the essence of you, the individual attributes that make you recognizable.

Together, your Name, Image, and Likeness form a triumvirate of personal branding power. And the recent NCAA NIL ruling has opened up new opportunities for student athletes like you to harness this power.

THE THREE PILLARS OF NIL: A DEEP DIVE

Understanding the three pillars of NIL—Name, Image, and Likeness—is the cornerstone of capitalizing on these new opportunities. Let's dive a bit deeper into each of these elements to understand their potential and implications in the world of student athletes.

1. NAME: THE POWER OF RECOGNITION

What's in a name? As it turns out, quite a lot. It is a badge of recognition and the cornerstone of your brand. In the realm of NIL, the value of your name ties directly into your reputation and achievements as an athlete. It's the label that fans cheer, the tag that reporters quote, and the brand that sponsors want to associate with.

However, understanding the potential of your name in this context also necessitates an understanding of the legal implications and potential pitfalls. Using your name for commercial purposes can be a double-edged sword. While it can generate income and build your personal brand, it can also lead to situations where you may need to protect your name legally. This means understanding copyright and trademark laws, privacy rights, and how they apply to the use of your name. All of which we will deep dive into in the *Understanding Intellectual Property Rights* section of this chapter.

2. IMAGE: THE VISUAL BRAND

Next is your image. In an age of visual media and social networks, your image holds immense potential. It's the face that appears on the poster, the figure that flashes across the TV screen, and the profile picture that represents you on social media. And with the new NIL rules, you now have the chance to monetize your image in ways that were previously unavailable to you as a student athlete.

Your image can be used in advertisements, product endorsements, social media campaigns, and more. And like your name, your image has legal protections and ramifications. Laws surrounding the right of publicity and defamation are particularly relevant here. Understanding these laws and knowing when to seek legal advice are crucial skills to have as you start to monetize your image.

3. LIKENESS: THE UNIQUE IDENTIFIER

Finally, your likeness. It's the combination of attributes that make you uniquely you. As we just mentioned, this could include your voice, your distinctive style, your signature move on the field, or even a catchphrase you're known for. Your likeness is a critical component of your brand and can be a powerful tool for differentiation in the marketplace. Given this, let's talk about your uniform number.

In the realm of sports, uniform numbers often become closely associated with the athletes who wear them. The number you wear on your jersey can become an iconic part of your brand, an instantly recognizable symbol that fans associate with you. For instance, basketball legend Michael Jordan's number 23 or soccer superstar Lionel Messi's number 10 have become synonymous with their identity and legacy. Thus, it is not uncommon for athletes to incorporate their uniform numbers into their personal branding strategies, using them in merchandise, promotional materials, and even their social media handles.

However, it's important to remember that the use of uniform numbers in commercial activities can present certain legal challenges. Depending on the league and the team you play for, there might be restrictions on how you can use your uniform number for personal profit. Therefore, it's crucial to understand your rights and obligations regarding the commercial use of your uniform number.

UNDERSTANDING INTELLECTUAL
PROPERTY RIGHTS

Do you have a brand? As you start to leverage your NIL, it is crucial to understand the role of intellectual property (IP) rights in establishing and protecting your brand. IP is a set of intangible assets that refer to creations of the mind. There are several different types of IP that are relevant and incredibly valuable for the monetization of your NIL. This includes copyrights, trademarks, your right of publicity, and your privacy rights.

Trademarks, patents, and copyrights can be registered through the United States Patent and Trademark Office (the "USPTO") and the United States Copyright Office which are federal agencies that have been established to help IP owners protect their IP. It is important to understand that you have inherent rights in your copyrights and trademarks, and they do not have to be registered with the USPTO or the US Copyright Office for you to have such rights. However, as we will discuss further below, there are numerous advantages to obtaining federal registration for your copyrights and trademarks. Generally, it is up to the rights' owner to protect his or her rights, and in some situations, the failure to protect certain IP rights can lead to the loss of the rights. The better you understand these IP rights, the more effectively you can use them to protect and monetize your NIL.

COPYRIGHTS

Let's start with copyrights. A copyright is a type of IP that protects original works of authorship that are fixed in a tangible medium. Anyone who creates an "original work," and "fixes" it, is a copyright owner. For a work to be considered "original," it must be created by a human author and be at least minimally creative. A copyright is considered "fixed" when it is captured in a medium such that the work can be perceived, reproduced, or communicated, for more than a short period of time. For example, copyrights include things such as photographs, graphics, works of art, books, music, songs, and other original works that are fixed in some tangible medium such as on paper, a record or CD, or even a digital audio file. In most situations, copyright protection lasts for the life of the author plus seventy years after the author's death. Once that time frame expires, the copyright then becomes part of what is known as the "public domain," which means that the copyright is no longer protectable, and anyone has the right to use the copyright.[1]

Understanding copyright means understanding that you own the rights to your original works as soon as they're fixed in a tangible medium. This means that you control how these works are used and who can use them. If someone

---

1   US Copyright Office, "What Is Copyright? | US Copyright Office," n.d., https://www.copyright.gov/what-is-copyright/.

uses your copyrights without your permission, they may be liable for copyright infringement which, generally, is when your original copyright is reproduced, distributed, performed, publicly displayed, or made into a derivative work without your permission.

You become a copyright owner as soon as your original work is fixed, even if it is not registered with the US Copyright Office. However, obtaining a federal registration for your copyrights has numerous advantages that you may want to explore with an intellectual property attorney. Specifically, in the US, in order to bring a copyright infringement lawsuit you must have a US copyright registration. Additionally, registration which is timely allows a copyright owner to obtain certain statutory damages and recover attorney's fees if the owner is successful in a copyright infringement claim against an infringing party. Additionally, owning a copyright registration is evidence of your copyright's validity which is a necessary means toward successfully defending your rights, and it creates a public record of your copyright that places the whole world on notice that you own and protect your copyrights.[2]

Copyright Fair Use

As we have shown you already, copyrights are a form of IP right that provides exclusive rights to the creators of

---

2   *Id.*

original works of authorship. However, the concept of "fair use" introduces a degree of complexity to copyright law.

Fair use is a legal doctrine that permits limited use of copyrighted material without obtaining permission from the rights owners. It is a defense against copyright infringement that, when applicable, allows others to use copyrighted material in certain situations. The Copyright Act specifies that the use of another's copyright is not considered an infringement if it is used "for purposes such as criticism, comment, news reporting, teaching (including multiple copies for classroom use), scholarship, or research."[3]

To determine whether the use of a copyright is a fair use, the Copyright Act instructs that a court should analyze four factors: (1) the purpose and character of the use, including whether such use is of a commercial nature or is for nonprofit educational purposes; (2) the nature of the copyrighted work; (3) the amount and substantiality of the portion used in relation to the copyrighted work as a whole; and (4) the effect of the use upon the potential market for or value of the copyrighted work.[4]

Here's where it gets tricky for student athletes. While you now have the rights to your NIL, certain uses of your copyrighted material may fall under fair use. For example,

---

3 17 U.S.C. §107.
4 *Id.*

a news outlet reporting on your game performance might use a photo of you without needing your explicit permission because the news outlet's use is considered fair use. Likewise, you need to be aware that the fair use defense is relatively limited in scope and often does not apply when a copyrighted work is used for any type of commercial purpose. Therefore, if you use copyrighted work without a license from the copyright owner, and such use is intended to help commercialize your NIL, there is a good chance your use of the work is not defensible as fair use. As you develop content, such as websites, blogs, etc. around your NIL you need to be aware of copyrights owned by others and the limits of the fair use defense.

Understanding the intricacies of copyrights and fair use is important because it helps you protect and monetize your creative works while respecting the rights of others. This will help you make informed decisions about how, when, and where your NIL may be used and not be classifiable as copyrighted material. The Copyright Fair Use Doctrine is a complex and highly specialized area of the law on which entire legal treatises have been written. Understanding the basics of copyright fair use, and the right questions to ask will be beneficial for your NIL business.

TRADEMARKS

It has been said that the hallmark of a protected property interest is the right to exclude others.[5] Trademarks are considered incredibly valuable property assets because the owner has the right to exclude others from using them.[6] A trademark is a word, phrase, symbol, or design that identifies and distinguishes the source of goods or services of one party from those of others. Trademarks distinguish the source of your goods or services from the goods or services sold by others; they signify that your goods or services are controlled by a single source and that they are of a certain level of quality, and they serve as a key part of your advertising and marketing efforts.[7] In simpler terms, a trademark is your "brand." This is how customers recognize businesses, products, and services in the marketplace, and what distinguishes a brand from its competitors.[8] For a student athlete, your name, signature, or even a catchphrase could be trademarked if it is "used in commerce," which means the trademark is used in connection with some product or service. By protecting

5   *College Sav. Bank v. Florida Prepaid Postsecondary Educ. Expense Bd.*, 527 U.S. 666, 673 (1999).
6   "A Trademark Is a Property Right," 1 McCarthy on Trademarks and Unfair Competition §2:10 (5th ed.).
7   "What a Trademark Does," 1 McCarthy on Trademarks and Unfair Competition §3:2 (5th ed.).
8   "Trademark Basics," USPTO, May 9, 2023, https://www.uspto.gov/trademarks/basics.

and policing your trademarks, you ensure that you have the exclusive right to use them for commercial purposes.

In essence, trademark law can protect your brand from being used by others in a way that might cause confusion about the source of goods or services. If someone uses your trademarked name, signature, or catchphrase without your permission, they may be liable for trademark infringement. It is important to note that we could teach an entire course on trademarks and branding alone. For a more in-depth knowledge and understanding of trademarks and branding, we recommend taking a full course on trademark law or intellectual property at your college or university. In this course, we are going to provide you with the background basics of NIL and branding so that you are generally aware of the legal and business issues surrounding NIL, and which professionals you should be hiring to assist you in creating your ultimate NIL enterprise.

This begs the question, How do you create a brand that is protectable? First, a trademark must be a tangible symbol, such as a word, name, symbol, device, or any combination of these things. Second, the trademark must be "distinctive," either because it is inherently distinctive, or through use over time, it has acquired the ability to distinguish your goods/services from those of others. Finally, the trademark must be used in commerce as a mark by a seller of goods or services. That is, it must identify and "distinguish" a seller's goods or services from those of the goods or services offered by others. In general, you want to pick a trademark that is a unique identifier of your brand and is distinct from any other existing trademarks.

Trademarks that are "inherently distinctive" are more easily protectable marks because they are protectable immediately upon first use. Fanciful, arbitrary, and suggestive words that are used as trademarks are considered "inherently distinctive." Other trademarks that merely describe the goods and services that they are used in connection with are considered "descriptive" and are not protectable unless they have acquired distinctiveness through use in commerce overtime—a concept known as "acquired distinctiveness."[9]

Fanciful trademarks are those marks that have been created for the sole purpose of functioning as a trademark and have no other meaning other than functioning as a trademark. An example of one of the strongest fanciful trademarks in the world is Starbucks. The Starbucks trademark is unique and has no other meaning other than serving as a source identifier for the iconic coffee brands. Arbitrary marks are those marks that have a known common meaning that have no association or relation to the goods or

---

9   "What Is a Trademark?," 1 McCarthy on Trademarks and Unfair Competition § 3:1 (5th ed.).

services being sold under them. One of the most iconic arbitrary brands in the world is Apple. An apple has a common meaning as the fruit that people eat, however, when used in connection with computers and smartphones, as Apple, Inc. does, the mark is inherently protectable as an arbitrary trademark. Suggestive marks are marks that suggest a quality or characteristic of the goods and services.[10] These marks are fairly common, and while they are not as strong as fanciful or arbitrary marks, they are still protectable trademarks. Examples of suggestive marks are Jaguar for automobiles (which suggests that the automobiles are as fast as an actual jaguar), and Netflix for a streaming service (which suggests movies or "flicks" that are streamed on the internet).[11]

Descriptive trademarks that "merely describe" the goods or services that they are used with do not initially serve as source-identifying marks and are not initially protectable under trademark law. However, as briefly mentioned earlier, descriptive trademarks can "acquire distinctiveness" by achieving "secondary meaning" through the use of the mark in commerce, or large amounts of advertising and marketing,

10 Barton Beebe, *Trademark Law an Open-Source Casebook*, version 8 (2021), accessed May 15, 2024, https://tmcasebook.org/wp-content/uploads/2021/07/BeebeTMLaw-v8-digital_edition.pdf.
11 "Suggestive Trademark," Mandour & Associates, March 2, 2020, https://www.mandourlaw.com/suggestive-trademark.

such that the mark is recognized by the consuming public as a brand. An example of a well-known descriptive trademark that has acquired distinctiveness and is a protected trademark is American Airlines for airline services.

It is important to note that marks that largely consist of surnames (or last names) are treated the same as descriptive trademarks and will only be protectable if they have acquired distinctiveness through use or widespread recognition.[12] A common example of such a mark is Ford for automobiles, which was created by Henry Ford. Not all of you reading this textbook will be able to protect trademarks in your name alone. It is important to consult an intellectual property attorney who specializes in trademark law prior to investing time and money in a trademark that may or may not be protectable.

How Do You Protect Your Trademarks?

In the United States, individuals or organizations that use a trademark in commerce establish enforceable rights in that mark regardless of whether the mark is registered on the Federal Trademark Register with the USPTO. The rights afforded an unregistered trademark are referred to as "common law" trademark rights. Therefore, you may already

---

12 Daniel A. Tysver, "Strength of Trademarks," BitLaw (2023), https://www.bitlaw.com/trademark/degrees.html.

own certain trademark rights, and you should be wary of relying only on what you can find on the Federal Trademark Register when evaluating rights held by others.

However, obtaining a federal trademark registration has numerous advantages that you will want to explore prior to investing time and money into your brand. First, securing a federal trademark registration with the USPTO gives you nationwide priority rights in your trademark over all other later users/registrants of marks that might cause confusion with yours.[13] Unregistered trademarks are only afforded protection in the geographic region in which they are actually used and possibly some limited zone of expansion. This means that, with a registered mark, as your brand begins to grow nationally, you can constrain prior users of highly similar marks to just the geographic region their trademarks are in use, and you can defend your mark from subsequent infringing uses all over the country.

Second, obtaining a registration is considered evidence of the mark's validity and your ownership of the mark.[14] This makes it more difficult for third-parties to contest the validity and ownership of your trademark.

Third, owning a federal trademark registration may allow you to obtain statutory damages and, in certain situations,

13 15 U.S.C. §1057.
14 *Id.*

attorney's fees against infringing and counterfeiting users of your trademarks if you are successful in defending your trademark in court.[15]

Fourth, only registered trademarks can achieve what is known as "incontestability status," which means that other trademark owners cannot attack the validity of your trademark if you have used it for five consecutive years in commerce, you made the necessary filings with the USPTO, there are no adverse decisions against you concerning your ownership of the trademark, and there are no pending claims questioning the ownership of your trademark.[16]

Finally, only registered trademarks can bear the recognized ® symbol, which serves as a notice to others of your rights. There are numerous other advantages to obtaining a federal trademark registration. If you plan on using your trademark and brand nationwide, it is advisable that you consider obtaining a trademark registration with the assistance of an intellectual property attorney before investing time and money into that trademark. You will want to specifically ask that the intellectual property attorney conduct a trademark screening search for your proposed trademark to determine if: (1) the mark you have chosen might infringe the prior rights of a third party, and (2) the mark is registrable

---

15   15 U.S.C. §1117(c).
16   15 U.S.C. §1065.

on the Federal Trademark Register, prior to investing time and money into the trademark.

Protecting your trademarks properly by following the sound advice of a trusted advisor such as an intellectual property attorney will provide your brand with immeasurable value. As your trademarks and brands become well-known, it will be important to have professionals effectively policing and protecting your brand from infringing and counterfeiting users of identical or highly similar trademarks who are attempting to capitalize on the goodwill of your brand.

We recognize that this is a lot to digest. There is a lot to know about trademarks, brand building, and protecting your IP assets. Now that you are aware of the basics of branding and the questions to ask, you should understand the importance of finding the right professionals to help you become a successful NIL entrepreneur. Hiring an attorney who specializes in trademark law can be an invaluable resource to you in creating and protecting your successful NIL brand. While hiring an intellectual property attorney is not free, investing in these professional services at the front end of your business venture will not only save you thousands of dollars in potential future legal fees should an issue arise with your NIL brand, but it is also a key investment in your NIL business that will help increase the value of your NIL business and recognition.

Competent intellectual property attorneys and sports agents can also help you negotiate NIL contracts on more favorable legal terms that capitalize on your NIL value while protecting your personal and business interests that you may not otherwise realize without professional guidance.

RIGHT OF PUBLICITY

Next, we have the right to publicity. This right protects you from having your Name, Image, or Likeness used for commercial purposes without your permission. This means that you control who can use your NIL and how they can use it.

The right of publicity varies from state to state in the US, but the overall principle is consistent: it protects you from the unauthorized commercial use of your NIL. Violations of this right can result in legal action.

PRIVACY RIGHTS

Lastly, we have privacy rights. While not traditionally viewed as intellectual property rights, privacy rights are critical in protecting your NIL. These rights protect you from unauthorized public disclosure of private facts, intrusion into your private life, false light privacy, and appropriation of your NIL for others' advantage.

Understanding these rights and how they apply to your NIL is essential in protecting your brand and maximizing your earning potential. However, it's also crucial to understand that these rights are nuanced, vary by jurisdiction, and often require legal expertise to navigate effectively.

KEY LEGAL CASES SHAPING NIL

While NIL legislation represents a groundbreaking shift in collegiate athletics, it did not come about in a vacuum. It is the result of several key legal cases that have shaped, and continue to shape, the landscape of NIL. Understanding these cases provides critical context to the current NIL rules and can give you a better understanding of how these rules might evolve in the future.

O'BANNON V. NCAA

Perhaps the most notable case in the context of NIL is *O'Bannon v. NCAA*. Ed O'Bannon, a former UCLA basketball player, brought the case forward when he discovered his likeness was being used in a video game without his permission or compensation.

In 2014, a US District Judge ruled in favor of O'Bannon, stating that the NCAA's regulations on amateurism, which prohibited student athletes from being compensated for the use of their NIL, violated antitrust laws. This ruling began to chip away at the NCAA's long-standing rules prohibiting athletes from benefiting from their NIL, setting the stage for the changes we see today.

However, it's worth noting the *O'Bannon* ruling didn't immediately lead to student athletes being able to monetize their NIL. It did, however, pave the way for further legal challenges to the NCAA's regulations and significantly contributed to the ongoing conversation about the rights of student athletes.

ALSTON V. NCAA

The *Alston* case, decided by the Supreme Court in 2021, built on the foundation set by the *O'Bannon* case. While this case didn't directly deal with NIL rights, it played a significant role in further challenging the NCAA's restrictions on student-athlete compensation.

Former West Virginia football player Shawne Alston and other student athletes filed the case, arguing that the NCAA's restrictions on education-related benefits violated antitrust laws. The Supreme Court ruled unanimously in favor of the athletes, stating that the NCAA could not restrict education-related benefits.

While this case did not directly lead to changes in NIL rules, it maintained the momentum of the *O'Bannon* case and increased pressure on the NCAA to reconsider its stance on student-athlete compensation, including NIL rights.

STATE NIL LAWS

Another pivotal development in the evolution of NIL rights is the enactment of state NIL laws. Starting with California's

Fair Pay to Play Act in 2019, several states have passed laws allowing student athletes to profit from their NIL.

These laws, which started taking effect in July 2021, played a significant role in pushing the NCAA to revise its NIL rules. The prospect of different rules applying to student athletes based on their state of residence created a situation that was unfeasible in the long term, contributing to the NCAA's decision to adopt a uniform policy allowing all student athletes to monetize their NIL.

TIME MANAGEMENT: PRIORITIZING NIL ACTIVITIES

As a student athlete, you're no stranger to juggling multiple responsibilities. Balancing academics, athletics, and personal life is a skill you've had to master. With the new NIL rules, you now have another component to add to the mix: managing your business and personal brand. To be successful on and off the field you must be able to prioritize being: (1) a student first and achieving a college degree, (2) a high-performing athlete, and (3) a successful entrepreneur running a business that could change you, and your family's life, forever.

Effectively managing your NIL activities involves strategizing, planning, and prioritizing. The key is to approach it as you would any other aspect of your life: with discipline, strategic thinking, and a clear set of attainable goals.

Start by defining your goals for your NIL activities. What do you hope to achieve by monetizing your NIL? Is it primarily about financial gain, or do you see it as a means to build your personal brand and lay the groundwork for your post-athletic career? Having clear goals will help guide your decision-making and keep you focused.

Be cautious not to spread yourself too thin. As the saying goes, "Just because you can, doesn't mean you should." Just because you can monetize your NIL in various ways, doesn't mean you should pursue every opportunity that comes your way. Evaluate each opportunity critically and don't be afraid to say no to opportunities that don't align with your goals or would spread your time and energy too thin.

At the same time, don't forget to make time for rest and relaxation. Balancing academics, athletics, and NIL activities is a significant undertaking, and it's important to avoid burnout. Ensure you set aside time to relax, spend time with friends and family, and engage in activities you enjoy outside of sports and work. Remember, maintaining a healthy work-life balance is key to your overall success and well-being.

To make the most of your NIL rights, combine your understanding of copyright and fair use with effective time management. With these skills in your toolkit, you'll be better equipped to navigate the world of NIL and leverage it to your advantage. You have the power to shape your future and build a legacy that goes beyond your career as a student athlete, and understanding these aspects of NIL is a crucial step on that journey.

The following chapters will provide more detailed insights into building your personal brand, negotiating deals, managing your finances, and more. As you continue to explore the potential of your NIL, remember that you are more than an athlete—you are an entrepreneur in the making. You are building a brand that can open doors to new opportunities and set the foundation for your post-athletic career. The power of your NIL is in your hands. So, stay disciplined, stay strategic, and get ready to unlock the power of your NIL.

TWO

THE SIGNIFICANCE OF COLLEGIATE ATHLETES

College campuses have been home to a plethora of note-worthy individuals, each contributing uniquely to the rich tapestry of academia. Among these individuals, college athletes have always held a pivotal role, standing out not just as students, but as multifaceted representatives of their institutions. Their place on campus is not merely about sports and competitions, it's much more intricate and far-reaching than that. They are the living, breathing embodiments of grit, competition, ambition, and perseverance.

THE HISTORICAL SIGNIFICANCE
OF COLLEGIATE ATHLETES

From the first intercollegiate football game in 1869 to today's high-profile, nationally televised games, college athletes have played an integral role in American sports culture. Athletes' performances on the field, court, or track have defined school rivalries, shaped local economies, and captivated audiences nationwide.

However, the significance of college athletes extends beyond their athletic prowess. They contribute to the academic life of their institutions, bring diversity to campus, and provide leadership to their peers. They demonstrate a level of dedication and discipline that sets them apart, balancing their commitments to their sport and their studies while developing the resilience and skills needed for success after graduation.

In many ways, collegiate athletes also act as ambassadors for their institutions. Their performances and conduct in the public eye can enhance a school's reputation, attract

prospective students, and boost the morale and unity of the student body and alumni community.

THE ECONOMIC SIGNIFICANCE OF COLLEGIATE ATHLETES

Economically, college athletes play a substantial role. Their performances draw large crowds, leading to ticket sales, merchandising, and broadcasting rights deals that generate substantial revenue for their universities and athletic conferences. For example, the NCAA's March Madness, College Football Playoff, and other prominent athletic events have been lucrative ventures, attracting millions of viewers and generating substantial profits.

However, until recently, college athletes have been largely excluded from this economic equation. The NCAA's strict rules regarding amateurism prohibited athletes from receiving any form of payment beyond their scholarships. This discrepancy between the revenue generated by college sports and the financial restrictions placed on the athletes themselves has been a subject of debate for years.

THE EVOLUTION OF NIL IN COLLEGE SPORTS

The recent shift in NIL rules marks a significant turning point in this debate. As of July 1, 2021, the NCAA adopted an interim policy allowing college athletes to monetize their NIL. This means that athletes can now earn money from endorsements, personal appearances, and their own creative ventures, marking a dramatic shift in the landscape of college sports.

The introduction of NIL rights in college sports has broad implications for college athletes. On a practical level, it offers athletes new opportunities for financial gain. For some, it might provide much-needed financial support. For others, it could present a path to wealth. Importantly, it also allows athletes to capitalize on a limited window of opportunity—while they are at their peak of popularity.

On a broader level, the evolution of NIL rights represents a shift in how we view college athletes. It acknowledges their economic value, empowers them with greater autonomy, and opens up new possibilities for them to build their personal brands.

However, as with any significant change, the new NIL rules also present challenges. Athletes must navigate complex issues related to contracts, intellectual property, and personal branding. They must balance their NIL activities with their existing academic and athletic responsibilities. And they must do all of this in an environment that is still figuring out how to adapt to these new rules.

Despite these challenges, the evolution of NIL in college sports is a promising development. It opens up new opportunities, evens the economic playing field, and empowers athletes with the rights to their names, images, and likenesses. It's a step toward acknowledging the significant role college athletes play, both on and off the field, and providing them with the autonomy and compensation they deserve.

THE FUTURE OF NIL IN COLLEGE SPORTS

As we look to the future, it's clear that NIL rights will continue to shape the landscape of college sports. The experiences of the first wave of athletes navigating these new rules will inform policies and best practices moving forward. Legal and legislative developments will continue to play a role, as will the efforts of athletes, institutions, and advocacy groups.

For student athletes, the evolution of NIL presents both exciting opportunities and new challenges. It's a chance to monetize your athletic and creative talents, build your personal brand, and set the groundwork for your future. But it's also a journey that requires understanding, strategic thinking, and careful navigation.

Monetizing your NIL comes with great opportunity and responsibility. You must also be aware of applicable state laws, NCAA compliance and conference-level NIL policies, and your college or university NIL policies. Taking the time to educate yourself on these policies will ensure that you are pursuing NIL activities in strict compliance. This means that you understand the appropriate laws, regulations, and policies. NIL violations could lead to the loss of your athletic eligibility and other steep penalties. Strict compliance with the rules is imperative for your success. You should be cautious and skeptical of NIL activities that feel like they do not comply with the rules. As a general caution, if someone approaches you to do a NIL deal that you are not sure complies with the rules and leaves you with questions, follow your gut and ask for help before you do anything that could jeopardize your career.

LANDMARK CHANGES IN NCAA NIL POLICIES

The journey toward NIL rights for student athletes has been long and convoluted, marked by landmark cases, policy changes, and a seismic shift in understanding the economic value of college athletes.

Historically, the NCAA's strict amateurism rules prohibited student athletes from profiting from their NIL. The NCAA held steadfast in its belief that allowing athletes to monetize their NIL would blur the lines between amateur and professional sports. Despite generating billions in revenue from college sports, the NCAA argued that allowing athletes to profit would compromise the integrity of collegiate sports.

However, pressure started mounting against the NCAA's restrictive policies. Public sentiment began to favor athletes' rights, and lawmakers introduced legislation at both the state and federal levels challenging the NCAA's NIL rules. At the time of this book's publishing, a federal law on NIL has not yet been signed into law. When that happens it may preempt state laws and the NCAA NIL policy to create a uniform standard on NIL across all fifty states. However, thirty-two states (and counting) have adopted state-level NIL laws that govern NIL activity in their respective states. Where a state law is silent on an issue, or where a state does not have a NIL law, the NCAA Interim NIL policy and the policy of your college or university will take priority. Understanding the basics of the differing laws, policies, and regulations that you have to comply with, and how they interact with each other, is the key to protecting yourself in a complicated NIL landscape.[17]

17 Philip J. Petrina, "Moving the Ball Forward on NIL: What Businesses and Student-Athletes Should Know," *The Legal Intelligencer*, April 20, 2023, https://www.law.com/thelegalintelligencer/2023/04/20/...

THE NCAA NIL POLICY BASICS

As discussed previously in July 2021, the NCAA adopted its Interim NIL Policy allowing student athletes to profit from their NIL. What does this mean? As a student athlete, your compliance with this policy is paramount. The basic tenet of the Interim NIL Policy is that student athletes may earn money off of their NIL in exchange for the student athlete's performance. Compliance with this policy is paramount. There must be some tangible deliverable on behalf of an entity that is wholly independent of the college or university that the student athlete attends. College or university coaches, staff members, employees, administrators, or any other person affiliated with your college or university may not be involved in your NIL activity. They may not procure or represent you in any aspect.[18] Specifically, the Interim NIL Policy prohibits:

- A NIL agreement without quid pro quo (e.g., compensation for work not performed). Student-athlete NIL agreements should include the expected NIL deliverables by a student athlete in exchange

---

...moving-the-ball-forward-on-nil-what-businesses-and-student-athletes-should-know/?slreturn=20240513094421.

18 "Name, Image and Likeness Policy Question and Answer," National Collegiate Athletic Association (February, 2023), https://ncaaorg.s3.amazonaws.com/ncaa/NIL/NIL_QandA.pdf.

for the agreed-upon compensation. Student athletes must be compensated only for work actually performed;

- NIL compensation that is contingent upon enrollment at a particular school. For example, institutions should not use NIL arrangements to improperly induce matriculation (e.g., guaranteeing a particular NIL opportunity upon enrollment);
- Compensation for athletic participation or achievement. Athletic performance may enhance a student athlete's NIL value, but athletic performance may not be the "consideration" for NIL compensation;
- Institutions providing compensation in exchange for the use of a student athlete's Name, Image, or Likeness.

NIL deals must not induce a "pay-for-play" scenario. That is, according to the Division I May 2022 NCAA Guidance, "NIL agreements must be based on an independent, case-by-case analysis of the value that each athlete brings to a NIL agreement as opposed to providing compensation or incentives for enrollment decisions (e.g., signing a letter of intent or transferring), athletic performance (e.g., points scored, minutes played, winning a contest), achievement (e.g., starting position, award winner) or membership on a team (e.g., being on roster)."

Most colleges, universities, and state laws require student athletes to disclose to the university their NIL activities prior to signing any NIL deal. These disclosure requirements are made to ensure that the NIL deal does not conflict with college and university policies and that it does not engage in activity that is prohibited by state law. Your compliance with these policies and disclosure requirements is tantamount to your NCAA eligibility. You should be sure to have NIL compliance discussions with the NCAA compliance officer at your college or university.

All of this NCAA compliance discussion leads us to another important topic: NIL collectives. You may be wondering, *What exactly is a NIL collective, and what role do they play in NIL deals?* NIL collectives are third-party, generally non-profit (in some cases for-profit) entities that have been established to promote and support specific NCAA institutions by making available NIL opportunities to prospective student athletes and student athletes of a particular institution. The laws, rules, and regulations surrounding NIL collectives and their operations are evolving and changing. However, NIL collectives currently exist independently of colleges and universities. They pool sponsors, money, and resources for a particular program's NIL activities and student athletes. NIL collectives can serve as a key resource for you in securing NIL deals. Establishing a relationship with the NIL collective for your program can help you achieve

NIL success. While NIL collectives are run independently of colleges and universities, they do trigger the NCAA's definition of a "booster." This means NIL collectives may not be involved in the recruiting process of prospective student athletes, and NIL deals with NIL collectives may not be guaranteed or contingent on initial or continuing enrollment at a particular institution.[19] As a general rule, you should never accept anything of value from a NIL collective (or a booster) without disclosing it to your college or university. You may not do this without a NIL agreement with the NIL collective or booster. This will protect you from potential NCAA infractions and rule violations if you are careful to ensure that you are performing a deliverable in exchange for anything of value provided to you by any third party and that such arrangements are memorialized in a written NIL agreement.

You should also be aware of the types of NIL deals that are prohibited by most state laws, as well as college and university policies. For example, you may not earn NIL compensation for activities involving a person, company, or organization related to or associated with the development, production, distribution, wholesaling, or retailing of any of the following:

---

19 "Interim Name, Image and Likeness Policy Guidance Regarding Third Party Involvement," National Collegiate Athletic Association (2022, May), https://ncaaorg.s3.amazonaws.com/ncaa/NIL/May2022NIL_ Guidance.pdf.

- Adult entertainment products and services;
- Alcohol products;
- Casinos and gambling, including sports betting, the lottery, and betting in connection with video games, online games, and mobile devices;
- Tobacco and electronic smoking products and devices;
- Prescription pharmaceuticals;
- A controlled dangerous substance; or
- Weapons, including firearms and ammunition.[20]

This section provides a general overview of the issues that you should be aware of and the types of questions that you should be asking as you engage in your NIL business. If you have questions about complying with these laws and regulations, you should be sure to ask your program's NCAA compliance officer or other college or university resources that your program makes available to you for help in complying with NIL laws and policies. The NCAA website is also another great resource with educational materials, like question-and-answer documents, that are available for you to increase your knowledge and understanding of NIL and comply with these confusing laws and policies. Hiring professional representation is also encouraged as a means of

20 24 Pa. Stat. § 20-2001-K.

protecting yourself and ensuring that you are taking adequate steps to comply with what has become a confusing and complicated landscape.

THE ECONOMIC IMPACT OF NIL
ON COLLEGIATE ATHLETICS

The economic impact of the new NIL policies on collegiate athletics is significant and multi-faceted. For student athletes, the new rules open up previously untapped revenue streams. Athletes can now secure endorsement deals, monetize their social media following, launch their own branded merchandise, and earn money from personal appearances and autograph signings.

This change has the potential to be particularly beneficial for athletes in non-revenue-generating sports or those who may not have professional career prospects. These athletes can leverage their college fame to secure financial stability during their college years and potentially beyond.

For universities, the economic impact is mixed. On one hand, the new NIL rules could potentially boost the attractiveness of their athletic programs, drawing in top talent and increasing their competitive edge. On the other hand, universities will need to invest in resources to educate and support athletes in navigating NIL deals, potentially adding to their operating costs.

For companies, the new NIL rules present fresh marketing opportunities. They can now tap into the popularity and influence of college athletes to promote their brands. This can be particularly impactful at a local level, where student athletes often have a strong fanbase.

Finally, for the economy as a whole, the new NIL rules stimulate economic activity. They encourage spending, create jobs, and foster entrepreneurship. They also add a new dynamic to the sports marketing industry, introducing fresh talent and new marketing opportunities.

However, the economic benefits of NIL rights are not automatic. They depend on the ability of athletes to effectively monetize their NIL and on the broader ecosystem's capacity to adapt to these new rules. From contract negotiation and legal considerations to personal branding and time management, athletes face a host of challenges in harnessing their NIL. Universities, companies, and legislators must also navigate this new landscape, balancing economic opportunities with the need for fair and ethical practices.

As you will see, navigating the world of NIL is not just about making money—it's about understanding the economic value of your skills and your brand, making informed decisions, and leveraging your NIL in a way that aligns with your values and long-term goals.

With the right approach, the economic impact of your NIL can extend far beyond your personal income. You can stimulate local businesses, inspire your peers, and make a positive impact on your community. You can redefine the economic significance of being a collegiate athlete and set a new precedent for future generations of student athletes.

RESOURCE MANAGEMENT: MAXIMIZING YOUR ATHLETIC AND ACADEMIC SUCCESS

Navigating the exciting and complex world of NIL while maintaining your commitments as a student and an athlete requires careful resource management. Your time, energy, focus, and even your physical well-being are resources that you need to allocate effectively to maximize your success both in athletics and academics.

Striking the right balance can be challenging. Monetizing your NIL can be time-consuming and emotionally taxing, involving negotiations, branding efforts, and personal appearances. However, it is crucial to remember that as a student athlete, your academic and athletic responsibilities remain paramount.

ACADEMIC SUCCESS

Your education is an important investment in your future. Many collegiate athletes will not go on to play their sport professionally, making their degree a crucial stepping stone to a successful career. Even for those who do pursue professional sports, having a degree provides a safety net and opens up opportunities for life after sports.

To balance your academic responsibilities with your NIL activities, consider the following strategies:

1. **Prioritize**: Make a list of your academic responsibilities and rank them based on urgency and importance. Prioritize tasks that contribute most significantly to your academic success.

2. **Time management**: Develop a daily or weekly schedule that allocates specific time slots for studying, attending classes, completing assignments, and preparing for exams. Be disciplined in sticking to your schedule.

3. **Get support**: Utilize academic resources provided by your university. This might include academic advisors, tutors, study groups, and online resources.

ATHLETIC SUCCESS

Your performance as an athlete plays a significant role in your ability to monetize your NIL. Maintaining your athletic performance requires time, energy, and commitment. Here are some strategies to help you manage your athletic responsibilities:

1. **Training**: Regular and effective training is crucial for maintaining and improving your performance. Schedule your training sessions and make them non-negotiable.

2. **Rest and recovery**: Allow ample time for rest and recovery to prevent injuries and maintain your physical and mental health.

3. **Nutrition**: Proper nutrition fuels your performance and recovery. Consider working with a nutritionist or utilizing nutritional resources provided by your university to develop a suitable eating plan.

MAXIMIZING YOUR NIL SUCCESS

To effectively monetize your NIL while maintaining your academic and athletic commitments, consider the following strategies:

1. **Brand building**: Develop a strong, authentic personal brand. This can increase your attractiveness to companies and reduce the time and effort required to secure endorsement deals.

2. **Strategic partnerships**: Choose partnerships that align with your brand and values. These are likely to be more profitable and satisfying in the long run.

3. **Professional advice**: Seek professional advice on legal, financial, and branding matters. This can prevent costly mistakes and maximize your earnings.

FROM COLLEGE TO PRO: THE NIL TRANSITION

The journey from collegiate athletics to professional sports is a monumental transition. If this is your desired path to take, you need to know that this transition is not just about a change in playing level; it's about moving from amateur status to a professional one, with increased responsibilities, expectations, and pressures. With the recent changes in NIL policies, there is now an additional layer of complexity in this transition—managing and maximizing your NIL as you make the leap from college to pro.

MANAGING YOUR NIL TRANSITION

The importance of effectively managing your NIL transition cannot be overstated. As a professional athlete, while the global visibility and prestige associated with professional sports offer increased marketing opportunities, your earning potential from NIL deals can still significantly matter. However, the stakes of transitioning are also higher, and the pitfalls of poor management can be costly.

Here are some strategies for managing your NIL transition:

1. **Education**: Equip yourself with knowledge about the professional sports industry, including contractual obligations, media rights, sponsorship opportunities, and the role of agents and managers. Understanding the landscape can help you make informed decisions and avoid potential pitfalls.

2. **Professional Representation**: As a professional athlete, the complexities of your NIL dealings will likely increase. Engaging a reputable agent or manager can be a valuable investment. They can negotiate deals on your behalf, offer advice, and ensure you are not being exploited.

3. **Brand Consistency**: As you transition to the professional level, your personal brand will evolve. It's crucial to maintain consistency and authenticity in your brand, as this is what fans and companies connect with.

4. **Network**: Building relationships within the professional sports industry can open up opportunities for NIL deals. This might include other athletes, company executives, marketers, and influential individuals in your sport.

5. **Legal Considerations**: As a professional athlete, you will likely encounter more complex legal issues related to your NIL. This might include contract disputes, intellectual property issues, and defamation claims. Investing in reliable legal advice is crucial.

6. **Financial Management**: The potential for increased earnings from NIL deals as a professional athlete brings with it the need for sound financial management. This includes budgeting, investing, tax planning, and managing cash flow. Financial education or engaging a financial advisor can be highly beneficial.

Don't worry, all these strategies for managing your NIL transition will be discussed in detail in later chapters of this book. By diving deeper into each of these topics, you will gain a comprehensive understanding of how to navigate the complexities of your NIL rights and make the most of the opportunities available to you while safeguarding your future.

MAXIMIZING YOUR NIL TRANSITION

While managing your NIL transition is crucial, it's also important to look at ways to maximize your NIL earnings as you transition to professional sports. Here are some strategies:

1. **Strategic Partnerships**: As a professional athlete, you will likely have access to more lucrative and high-profile NIL opportunities. However, not all deals are created equal. Look for partnerships that

align with your brand, offer fair compensation, and have the potential for long-term collaboration.

2. **Social Media Presence**: Your social media platforms are a valuable tool for promoting your brand and securing NIL deals. As you transition to professional sports, consider how you can grow and leverage your social media presence.

3. **Entrepreneurial Ventures**: Your status as a professional athlete can open up opportunities for entrepreneurial ventures, such as launching your own branded merchandise, starting a sports training clinic, or even creating a nonprofit organization.

4. **Media Opportunities**: From interviews to guest appearances, media opportunities can enhance your visibility, boost your brand, and open up further NIL opportunities.

Again, stay tuned, as in the upcoming chapters, we'll delve deeper into these areas, equipping you with the insights you need to master your NIL transition and thrive in the world of professional sports. As you step into this new stage of your career, remember: you're not just an athlete; you're an entrepreneur, and the power of your NIL is in your hands. Harness it wisely, and you'll unlock opportunities that extend far beyond the playing field.

CASE STUDIES:
COLLEGIATE ATHLETES EXCELLING IN NIL

To conclude Chapter Two, we shall look at practical cases that may inspire you and start to get you warmed up to the potential you hold. Since the adoption of the new NIL rules, several collegiate athletes have demonstrated how to navigate this landscape successfully. Here are some case studies:

1. **Spencer Rattler**: Rattler, a quarterback at the University of Oklahoma, was among the first athletes to launch his own branded merchandise line after the NCAA's new NIL policies came into effect. Rattler's approach demonstrates the potential of using your NIL to create your own products and directly profit from them.

2. **Haley and Hanna Cavinder**: The Cavinder twins, basketball players at the University of Miami, leveraged their large TikTok and Instagram following to secure several endorsement deals. The Cavinders show how athletes can use social media to monetize their NIL.

3. **D'Eriq King and McKenzie Milton**: These two football players partnered to create Dreamfield, a company that aims to help other student athletes monetize their NIL. Their story illustrates the entrepreneurial opportunities that the new NIL rules can unlock.

These athletes have demonstrated the power and potential of NIL. They have effectively leveraged their talents, fame, and entrepreneurial spirit to maximize their NIL earnings while maintaining their athletic and academic commitments.

Their success, however, did not come without challenges. They had to learn how to balance their NIL activities with their academic and athletic responsibilities. They had to navigate complex legal and financial issues, and they had to build and maintain their personal brands.

However, these athletes also had support systems in place. They had advisors, mentors, and resources to help them navigate the NIL landscape. They also had discipline, strategic thinking, and a clear understanding of their values and goals.

The key takeaway from these case studies is this: Successfully monetizing your NIL is achievable, but it requires a strategic approach, a robust support system, and a commitment to maintaining your academic and athletic performance.

As a student athlete, you have a unique set of challenges and opportunities. But with the right strategies and resources, you can effectively manage your responsibilities, maximize your NIL earnings, and set yourself up for long-term success.

Whether you are just starting to explore the potential of your NIL or you are already well on your way to building your brand and securing deals, remember this: Your journey is your own. Your experiences, values, and goals will shape your approach to NIL. And with every step you take, you are paving the way for future generations of student athletes.

In the coming chapters, we will delve deeper into the strategies, skills, and resources you need to successfully navigate the world of NIL. But for now, remember this: The power of your NIL lies not only in your athletic talent and fame but also in your ability to balance your responsibilities, make informed decisions, and stay true to your values and goals.

THREE

PREPARING FOR NIL

s you have seen, as a collegiate athlete, one of your most valuable assets is your NIL. However, to unlock the full potential of your NIL, you need a clear, strategic plan. This chapter focuses on the importance of having a personal NIL strategy and provides a roadmap for developing one.

THE IMPORTANCE OF A PERSONAL NIL STRATEGY

The potential to earn income or create assets from your NIL is an exciting prospect. However, it's not without its challenges. Monetizing your NIL involves navigating complex legal, financial, and branding issues. It requires balancing your NIL activities with your academic and athletic commitments.

Perhaps most importantly, it requires making strategic decisions that align with your values and long-term goals.

Before committing to a NIL business, the candidate should be prepared to be a student first, an athlete second, and a student-athlete business owner last. From our collective experience, many student athletes are prepared to be an athlete first in most cases because they are passionate about their sport. The reason the mindset has to be student first is as of this writing there are academic standards high school athletes and collegiate athletes must maintain in the classroom in order to perform competitively in their respective sports. So, if high school or collegiate athletes do not take care of their academics, no one can take care of the athlete because they will not play competitively if they become ineligible. If the athlete cannot play, they cannot reach their full athletic potential on their respective stage to leverage a NIL business revenue opportunity effectively or efficiently. Collectively, we all hope your NIL brand would promote the student-first mentality. Why? What if you are limited in competitive action due to factors out of your control, such as coaching decisions or injury? Adopting the student-first mentality is not just good for NIL, but for the rest of your life and all areas of life when you approach with a desire to learn. The game leaves our bodies, but not our minds. The NIL strategy must be more than just a sport; it must be your personal purpose or your "why" story. The feature is what you do, and what people are inspired by is your story. The people buy your story or your brand to become your raving fans. Think about the 1990s movie about Rudy, the underdog walk-on at Notre Dame. They made a movie about the "why" of the person and people bought it, and as viewers, we never felt sold. People wanted to pay for the experience of the story on the silver screen. That is the power of knowing your "why."

A personal NIL strategy can guide you in navigating these challenges and making informed decisions. It can help you identify opportunities that align with your brand and values, prioritize your time and energy, and navigate legal and financial issues. It can also provide a roadmap for building your personal brand, securing beneficial partnerships, and managing your earnings effectively.

Furthermore, a personal NIL strategy can help you maintain your eligibility and integrity as a student athlete. By setting clear boundaries and making informed decisions, you can ensure that your NIL activities comply with NCAA rules and uphold the standards of your university and athletic program.

In short, a personal NIL strategy is not just about maximizing your earnings—it's about navigating the world of NIL in a way that aligns with your values, protects your interests, and sets you up for long-term success. Developing a personal NIL strategy involves several steps. Here's a roadmap to guide you.

SELF-ASSESSMENT

Before you can develop an effective NIL strategy, you need to understand your strengths, interests, and values. What are your unique skills and attributes? What are you passionate about? What are your personal and professional goals?

Your answers to these questions can guide you in developing your personal brand, identifying potential partnerships, and setting boundaries for your NIL activities. For example, if you're passionate about community service, you might prioritize partnerships with companies that share this value. Or, if you're interested in a career in broadcasting, you might focus on building your media presence.

MARKET ANALYSIS

Understanding the landscape of NIL opportunities can help you identify lucrative and satisfying opportunities. This involves researching companies that sponsor collegiate athletes, understanding what these companies are looking for in athletes, and identifying trends in the industry. A market analysis can also help you understand your worth in the market and negotiate fair compensation for your NIL activities.

PERSONAL BRANDING

Your personal brand is a crucial component of your NIL strategy. It's what makes you unique and attractive to companies and fans. Developing your personal brand involves identifying your unique traits and values, creating a consistent image and message, and building a strong presence on social media and other platforms.

PARTNERSHIP STRATEGY

Your partnership strategy involves identifying potential partners, understanding what they can offer you, and negotiating deals that benefit both parties. A good partnership strategy also involves setting boundaries for your partnerships. This includes defining what types of partnerships you are comfortable with, what types of activities you are willing to engage in, and what compensation you expect.

There are effectively two partnership teams a NIL student-athlete must consider. Your customers and your team of professional advisors. Who are your customers? They could be your followers and fans on social media platforms, corporate sponsors, and/or people buying your apparel as an example. How you treat your customers matters. Think of the corporate sponsors you want to align with your NIL brand and how those sponsors will compensate you for the earned media or have a give back strategy to the corporate sponsor through social media platforms. Consider a fit process from your perspective and from the sponsors'. Not all sponsors want to partner with one athlete. As an example, are you willing to offer a team deal and help your teammates?

Regardless, there will have to be a contract between your NIL Business and the sponsor to remain compliant.

The second part of partnership strategy is building your team of trusted professional services partners. This can be your attorney and their law firm of different legal specialties needed including your CPA, your financial advisor, your endorsement agent, or anyone that is bound by law to put your best interests first when collaborating with you or representing you. If they do not hold a license to practice their services be extremely cautious. These partners are people and/or organizations that you will have to partner with and pay for their respective services beyond your capability due to specialization needs and/or your lack of time. We cannot stress enough this is not a business venture you should venture on a self-directed basis due to the complexity of rules and offerings that may or may not be in the best interest of you or your school. Having a trusted team of advisers for legal, tax, endorsements, and finance are crucial to the sustainability of a NIL business. Think of them as your coaches. Do the best professional athletes have private coaches? Of course, do they do, so why not have the same for your business and your personal financial achievements? We are never successful alone.

A NIL student-athlete and their respective families might think there is not a need for certain professionals. However, a good practice is to seek them out, so they are on your bench ready to call up when you need them. How do you ask? If you are collaborating with an attorney, CPA, or financial advisor in the process they have a network of the professionals they refer and work with on a regular basis. Because as your NIL business grows it is inevitable the complexity will too and the need for good partners in your corner with wisdom and credentials will soon follow if you are successful. The various professionals are there to help you navigate the complexities for you or with you so that you can stay focused on being you and pursuing your why. We will address best practices on how to interview and evaluate these types of partners before you hire them.

EXAMPLES OF HOW PROFESSIONAL PARTNERS ARE IMPORTANT

There are often examples or cases that better illustrate the importance and the purpose of the use of professionals. We cannot stress enough; it is ok to be oblivious to the rules and laws while in high school or college as to how to operate business processes and how various rules work. Think federal laws, FTC, SEC, IRS, DOL, State NIL Laws, and NCAA rules and regulations. We can assure you; a do-it-yourself approach is not something we recommend with NIL by any of the professional contributors and authors of this book. When it comes to rules or laws, it is not what you know, it is what you should know. Here we outline two case examples based on real events to illustrate how ambitious student athletes, generous sponsors, and well-meaning collectives can create risks for the student-athlete without a team of professionals in place to assist. Both cases are similar in how a student-athlete formed a direct relationship with a local business owner while they were in high school and then made it to the highest levels of college athletics. The sport and names are irrelevant; it is the sequence of choices and the ignorance of the rules that potentially put the student-athletes at risk or their athletic institutions at risk until there was proper professional intervention. Both cases completed ethically or not done at all.

CASE EXAMPLE 1

- Local business owner is a large supporter of the high school team's booster club. Befriends the star player in high school and builds a genuine friendship with the student athlete and becomes a mentor.
- Student Athlete gets a full ride scholarship to a division 1 NCAA school and begins to show promise in their sophomore year with national recognition.
- Business owner offers to pay for a lease of a luxury vehicle for the student-athlete because he wants to be generous and help.

- Car dealership takes a credit application from the student-athlete and is prepared to co-sign the business owner.

What were the potential issues the student athlete would have known if they had a team of professional partners?

1. Potential NCAA infractions on gifting rules if the promotional lease deal was not set up correctly between the student-athlete and the business owner through a NIL contract. This must be a written contract by an NIL attorney licensed by the state where the student attends college. The deal can be done between a sponsor and the student athlete, but the agreement must be compliant.

2. Tax implications of receiving a lease as a sponsorship. The value of the lease is imputed income under the Internal Revenue Code.

3. Will the student-athlete have the cash to pay the tax on the imputed income?

4. Who is paying the car insurance? It is the responsibility of the recipient.

5. Student-athletes do not have credit and a turndown could further damage the student athlete's credit rating. There is a proper way to build credit and applying for the loan with a cosigner could be a way to establish credit, but in this case, it would have created an NCAA infraction.

6. Student-athletes did not have enough income to qualify for the lease of $1,000 per month. Co-signing for the student-athlete and the sponsorship by the business owner would have both been on the hook financially. What if they have a falling out?

7. Where is the NIL contract between the business owner and the student-athlete that outlines what the student-athlete is going to do in return to qualify as a NIL deal? What does the media give back to the sponsor from the student-athlete? The contract spells this out. There is disclosure to various governing bodies.

Fortunately, this potential public relations crisis was averted when the legal, tax, and financial professionals were brought into the situation to assist the student-athlete and the sponsor. The dealership and the business owner had to look over the facts regarding the promotional lease deal properly with the car dealership paid for by the business owner in exchange for earned media by the student athlete through a NIL contract.

CASE EXAMPLE 2

Prominent business owner and sponsor of a college sports program wanted to sponsor a student-athlete they knew recently committed to the college shortly after NIL rules passed by the NCAA. The offer was a generous six figure deal to the student-athlete through the college's respective collective. This was a four-year deal to the student-athlete over four years.

In this case the NIL Collective collects the money from the corporate sponsor and sets up the student-athlete on appearance deals for the corporate sponsor's events with a NIL contract. The Collective issues the student-athlete a 1099 with 20 percent Federal tax withholding. The student-athlete did not have a business entity established.

What were the potential issues the student athlete would have known in advance if they had a team of professional partners?

1. Have a business entity established with a business bank account.

2. They would have negotiated earned media instead of time commitment which the student-athlete did not have for appearances.

3. Hire a CPA, NIL Business attorney, and a licensed financial advisor.

4. Set up a retirement account through the student-athlete NIL business to make pre-tax contributions to reduce tax burden and save money for the student-athletes future.

5. Proper income tax withholding or quarterly payments for federal single filer status, state income tax, and FICA payroll taxes to avoid penalty if not paid by January 15 of the following year.

Did the student athlete set aside enough for quarterly tax payments to federal and state governments?

Collectives must choose to assist student-athletes with referring or paying for professional advisors. In this case at the time of the first payment the Collective did not. Under NCAA rules the colleges and universities cannot pay for the services of professionals, but the Collectives can if they so choose. We understand student-athletes and their families may not have the resources to hire professionals which is why professional service firms are looking into ways to do pro-bono work selectively or payment for their services once there is revenue as they might structure for other start-up companies that are clients in other industries.

These case examples reinforce the three core business administration strategies to be aware of when starting your NIL business. A wonderful way to help you visualize the importance is a football analogy. Can the football game start without the kickoff and kickoff return teams? Of course not! Think of your special teams as the legal and tax professionals to help you kick off your business venture, so you can provide a return to yourself in the form of income legally and tax effectively. Why would anyone start a business without their special teams for legal, tax, and financial in place? Sadly, often people do, and tax and legal professionals need to be brought in soon enough or it can lead to greater costs and stresses due to the potential challenges created with governing bodies. Setting up your business with sound legal and tax infrastructure through tax and legal professionals is the best start-up sunk cost you can make in yourself. Check with your Collective or booster club if this is something they are willing to do to support you.

It is your job and responsibility as the business owner to communicate to these professionals. As professionals they will be transparent about rules and regulations that go beyond your scope of understanding. For example, have you read the state laws on business formation in your state or the state you are attending college? These types of laws may prevent you from doing it the way you want. However, the professionals are often able to help you structure and set up your business effectively so you can make as much as you want legally.

These professionals all come with a financial investment. Please realize those costs are far cheaper to set up and maintain the business properly than it is to pay to fix problems without these structures in place from the beginning. As professionals, contributing to this book, this is why we are here to help student-athletes avoid the pitfalls that can arise quicker than any of them may ever realize legally, tax wise with the IRS, state laws, governing athletic associations, and/or the state tax revenue department. These rules are public, but are not common knowledge, especially if you are not in pursuit of a business administration, accounting, or pre-law learning degrees.

Our goal as contributors with regards to the Legal, Tax, and financial strategies is to share more about the awareness of what is important to consider before accepting the first dollar to your business. There may have been you have been to a business, like a diner or a retail store, where the business owner frames and hangs up their first dollar earned. Not too much can we purchase for $1 USD anymore, but as contributors to this book we really would like you to consider what this means. The first dollar you could earn with your NIL business do not take for granted, because the second dollar earned is not a guarantee. Being aware of what it takes to get a business up and running will also help you appreciate and find gratitude for the first dollar(s) earned. We are aware of cases of student-athletes turning down $50,000 sponsorships because they thought it was not enough and when their sport's season started, they did not have a sponsor. The only way to ensure the second dollar and beyond is to follow basic principles in business. The strategies that follow are the foundations for your business administration mindset as an entrepreneur.

FINANCIAL AND LEGAL STRATEGY

Our purpose as contributors, is to bring forward the financial and legal issues you must be aware of as you prepare for your NIL business. Awareness is the first step for you. Our goal as professionals contributing to this book is to share our knowledge based on years of practicing experience with business owner clients in our respective fields. This includes accredited certifications and degrees specific to our fields, with recent NIL experiences with NCAA Division I student-athletes. These issues may seem foreign to you and that is ok because you will have hired or retained professionals on your team before venturing too far in your NIL business. We hope you do it for your sake and the reputation of your school. These are topics and issues to be aware of to help you think for yourself and be aware of the issues to talk with your respective financial and legal advisors. These topics are complex and beyond the scope of this book. Like most investors, if you are hiring a financial professional you will lean on them to help you decipher the complexities into terms you can understand to make the appropriate decisions that serve your best interests, not theirs. You can never ask a dumb question to any professional. You are not there to impress them as to how smart you are by acting like you already know. Professionals are compensated to answer your questions from their deep understanding in terms you can comprehend to lead you to decisions that serve your best interests now and hopefully for the future.

Your financial strategy involves managing your earnings effectively, including budgeting, investing, and tax planning. It also involves understanding and negotiating contracts to ensure you are receiving fair compensation and protecting your rights.

Your legal strategy involves understanding the legal implications of your NIL activities. This includes intellectual property laws, state level NIL laws, NCAA compliance policies and rules, and university compliance policies. It also involves securing reliable legal advice to help you navigate these complex issues.

THE BASICS OF INCOME TAX AND
CREATING A TAX STRATEGY

Hiring a Certified Public Accounting (CPA) firm will be one of the most important first decisions you can make as a business owner. The CPA firm you search to hire will need to offer start-up business advisory services, payroll tax coordination and tax preparation. You will need a CPA firm that will help you set up bookkeeping software, payroll services, offer business advice around best practices, and often will have a start-up administration checklist for you to follow. You cannot think of everything on your own without this expertise. If you make the money before engaging the CPA, engage a firm as soon as possible before you spend any of what you just earned. We understand that sometimes the opportunity may come to you before you have your team in place.

You will need to communicate to the CPA the retail platform you are selling apparel due to state sales tax, any royalty agreements you have set up, share your endorsement contracts, and anything they ask for to provide you the best service. Any dollar that flows through your business the CPA is there to help you determine whether it is revenue or an expense and what is taxable to federal, state, and local tax bureaus. As a small business owner, think of your CPA as your Chief Financial Officer or your corporate finance team.

The costs for these services are far cheaper than paying for an actual CFO at this stage of your business. Not to be overly redundant, keep in mind when you must find a CPA, Attorney or financial professional first they often can be great resources to refer you to the other professional you need. These three groups of professionals tend to collaborate with shared clients and often meet with the clients depending upon the situation. The CPA often is one of the most trusted and core members of your professional team.

In summary you need your CPA for:

- Startup Business checklists
- Business Services and Advice for Best Practices
- Payroll Services
- Bookkeeping
- Tax Preparation and Advice

FINANCIAL STRATEGY

We have covered awareness with regards to potential tax and legal issues to consider and coordinate with the respective professionals. When it comes to earning money, there is knowledge that is worth pursuing regardless of your interests. In other words, not all of you will pursue an education in business, but if you are going to own a NIL business there are pertinent topics to be aware of to learn about and embrace as a business owner. You do not need to become an expert in each, but learning enough to be aware about each issue can make you a better business owner and help you grow personally and professionally.

What we are about to share here will make any academic adviser cringe, but when Steve Jobs was still alive, he spoke about taking courses that interested him, during his Stanford University commencement speech. It was not just about what pertained to any one degree. So regardless of where you are in your education journey, these are the topics worth exploring as a business owner or what we call Business Literacy Topics.

Student Athlete Biz Education Topics to Explore
- Entrepreneurship
- Risk Management
- How to make an idea into revenue that is profitable
- Time and Energy Management
- Exit Planning Strategy Resources
- Twelve Competencies in running a business.
- Value Acceleration Methodology process
  - wealth gap
  - profit gap
  - value gap
- How to make revenue profitable with growth
  - phases of a business
  - how to build a team for your business

- Accountability: Person in the mirror
- Discipline: Creating good financial and business habits

The third part of the financial strategy after you have your legal advice, tax planning, and business planning underway is financial literacy. Think of this as what you do with the money after your customer has paid you and you have paid tax or have a chance to save before taxes. Think of this as your take home pay after all expenses and taxes.

Here are the issues you will want to cover, coordinate, and implement with your financial advisor.

Student Athlete Financial Literacy

- Liquidity/Liability Management
  - Cash and Credit Management
  - Emergency Fund
  - Establishing credit
  - Budgeting
- Retirement—think funding.
  - Owner only 401(k)
  - Professional League 401(k)
  - Professional League Pension
  - Simple IRA Plan
  - SEP IRA
  - Roth

- Traditional non-deductible contributions converted to Roth IRAs if earnings exceed the limits.
- These strategies will need coordination during the college years and their professional years when paid by a team in the various professional leagues.
- Insurance: Life, Disability, Liability—These are complex insurance products and topics but need to consider even at a student athlete's early age. You will want to talk with your financial professional to determine what is in your best interest to consider and how to get the proper amounts of insurance in-force and make sure there is sustainable income to afford policies going forward to protect you and your business.
- Estate Planning—Your financial advisor can speak to the generalities but will need to coordinate with an estate attorney of your resident state to design and implement.
  - Executor of your Will, POA, Directives of Health Care/Living Will—Who do you trust and who can manage these fiduciary responsibilities for you? Is this person willing to serve in these various roles?
  - Trust Planning
  - Gifting/Leaving a legacy.

- Gifting During Lifetime
  - Charity
  - Family
- Investments—This is where your advisor will be extremely valuable to help you with a financial plan and work with you on the various aspects of how to allocate money in different investment products that are most appropriate for your long-term goals across distinct types of investment vehicles.
  - Mutual Funds—thousands to choose from
  - Exchange Traded Funds—thousands to choose from
  - Passive versus Active Investing Strategies
  - Annuities—these are insurance contracts that can promise income at a future age.
  - SEC Registered Alternative Investments—this is for higher net worth, but important to understand compared to non-registered alternatives that have been known to get professional athletes into bad investments historically.
  - Individual Stocks/Equities
  - Fixed Income vehicles i.e., bonds, Certificates of Deposit.

HIRING PROFESSIONALS SUMMARY

As we have shared, finding the legal and tax professionals is your first step. Whichever professional you interview first they can make a referral to others when asked. It is standard practice to interview at least three business attorneys, CPAs, and financial advisors. Why? Because the one you interview is not a fit. We tend to do business with people we like and trust. Not everyone is going to be a fit. Cost is always an issue in the absence of value. Before engaging in consultative dialogue about your situation. Professionals often will have websites that describe the services and areas of practice. As professionals contributing to this book, we typically see the professionals talk about their firm's capabilities, their personal areas of practice, their process in helping you, how they get paid, and hopefully their "why." In summary, you will want to know Why they do what they do, what they do, how they do it, and how they get paid. Listen for these specific items and if the professional in question do not address those questions these are the questions to ask. After interviewing three professionals in each area of focus, legal, tax, and financial, you will have a clear idea who you will be most comfortable with based upon those answers. They should then be asking you what is important to you. These professionals may already have a list of issues for you to look over, or a checklist to understand what you might or might not have in place. If they do not, then they should be asking you these types of questions. There is not a right or wrong, it will be a difference in style across industries and firm professionals. If they do not share on their websites or do not clearly spell things out ask Why they do what they do, how they do it, and how they get paid.

How professionals receive compensation varies profession to profession. Attorneys typically charge an hourly rate. CPAs may charge an hourly rate or a flat fee for services plus an hourly rate for work over and beyond the flat fee scope of work. Financial professionals have much more complicated compensation arrangements. Bank accounts for example you will want to inquire if there are fees and if there is interest rate sweep feature on the business account. For the financial advisor they may charge commissions per transaction under the 1934 Act and/or if they work under the 1940 Adviser Act and charge a percentage of the assets you have under management. Financial Advisors can charge commissions for securities transactions. Financial professionals at regional or national broker dealer firms have the capability to do both, but not in the same type of account. Independent Advisors or Registered Investment Advisors may charge commission, percentage of assets they manage, and Financial Advisors may charge an hourly rate or flat fee for certain types of planning. This is why interviewing different professionals is so important. Gathering this information is so important in making the decision.

Across all three professions look for credentials of the professionals beyond the basic licenses as it is a sign they are deeply committed to learning and to growth in their area of practice to be the better advisor for you.

The Why, the What, and processes will vary amongst professionals and here are follow-up questions to ask to better understand if they are a fit for you:

1. What has your experience been with start-up business owners and for NIL?
2. How will we communicate and how often will we meet?
3. How will I be billed for the services?
4. How does your process work?
5. Are there existing clients like me that I can speak to understand what it is like to collaborate with you?

TIME MANAGEMENT STRATEGY

Balancing your NIL activities with your academic and athletic responsibilities is crucial. A good time management strategy can help you prioritize your time and energy, avoid burnout, and maintain your performance on and off the field.

IMPLEMENTATION AND EVALUATION

Once you have your NIL strategy in place, the next step is to implement it. This involves actively seeking out partnerships, promoting your personal brand, and managing your time and resources effectively.

Equally important is evaluating your strategy regularly. This involves assessing your progress, identifying challenges, and adjusting your strategy as needed. Regular evaluation can help you stay on track with your goals, learn from your experiences, and continuously improve your NIL strategy.

THE POWER OF A PERSONAL NIL STRATEGY

Developing and implementing a personal NIL strategy can be a complex process, but the potential rewards are well worth the effort. With a well-thought-out strategy, you can maximize your NIL earnings, protect your rights and interests, and set yourself up for long-term success.

But perhaps the greatest benefit of a personal NIL strategy is the sense of control and empowerment it can provide. By taking a proactive, strategic approach to your NIL, you're not just reacting to opportunities as they arise—you're actively shaping your future. You're not just an athlete; you're an entrepreneur, and your NIL is your ticket to an exciting, rewarding entrepreneurial journey.

Remember, your NIL is more than just a source of income—it's a reflection of who you are. It's a platform for expressing your values, showcasing your talents, and making an impact. And with a strong NIL strategy, you can leverage this platform to its full potential.

BUILDING YOUR NIL BRAND: A STEP-BY-STEP GUIDE

Building a brand around your NIL is one of the essential aspects of maximizing your value as an athlete. Your brand is your identity to the outside world; it encapsulates your values, your passions, and your unique talents, and it is what sets you apart from other athletes. It's what makes companies want to associate with you and fans want to support you. In short, it's one of your most valuable assets.

Here is a step-by-step guide to building your NIL brand:

1. Identify Your Unique Attributes

Start by identifying what sets you apart from other athletes. What unique skills or traits do you possess? What are your passions? What experiences have shaped you? These attributes will serve as the foundation of your brand.

2. Define Your Brand Message

Your brand message is a concise statement that communicates what you stand for and what you bring to the table. It should reflect your unique attributes, your values, and your vision. Your brand message will guide your branding activities and serve as a point of connection with your fans and potential partners.

3. Create a Consistent Brand Image

Consistency is key in branding. From your logo and colors to your voice and style, all aspects of your brand should be consistent across platforms. This helps to build recognition and trust with your audience.

4. Build Your Online Presence

Your online presence is a critical part of your brand. This includes your social media profiles, website, and any other online platforms where you engage with fans and potential partners. Ensure that all your online platforms reflect your brand image and message consistently.

5. Engage Your Audience

Engaging with your audience is a powerful way to build your brand. This can include interacting with fans on social media, sharing behind-the-scenes content, or hosting events. Remember, your brand is not just about you—it's about your audience too.

6. Align with Companies That Reflect Your Brand
The companies you choose to associate with can have a significant impact on your brand. Choose partners that align with your brand values and image, and can help you reach your target audience.

7. Continuously Monitor and Adjust Your Brand
Branding is not a one-time activity. As you grow and evolve, so should your brand. Continuously monitor your brand's performance, seek feedback from your audience, and adjust your brand as necessary.

By following these steps, you can build a strong, authentic brand that resonates with your audience, attracts beneficial partnerships, and maximizes your NIL value. Remember, your brand is an extension of yourself. It's a reflection of who you are, what you stand for, and what you bring to the table. Make it count.

AGENTS AND MANAGERS: SELECTING THE RIGHT REPRESENTATION

As your NIL value grows, so does the complexity of managing it. At some point, you may consider engaging an agent or manager to help navigate this complexity. This individual or agency will play a crucial role in negotiating contracts, identifying opportunities, and managing your brand. Therefore, selecting the right representation is a critical decision.

FACTORS FOR SELECTING AN AGENT OR MANAGER

1. Experience and Expertise

Look for an agent or manager who has experience in the sports industry and a deep understanding of NIL policies. They should be well-versed in contract negotiation, brand management, and legal issues related to NIL.

2. Reputation

The reputation of your agent or manager can significantly impact your brand. Do some research on potential agents or managers. Look for any red flags, such as legal issues or disputes with previous clients.

3. Alignment with Your Goals and Values

Your agent or manager should align with your goals and values. They should understand your vision for your career and brand and be committed to helping you achieve it. In addition, they should respect your boundaries and support your academic and athletic commitments.

4. Transparency and Communication

A good agent or manager should be transparent and communicative. They should keep you informed about potential opportunities, contracts, and any issues that arise. They should also be open to your questions and concerns and provide clear, honest answers.

5. Services and Fees

Understanding what services an agent or manager provides and how they charge for these services is crucial. Be sure to discuss this upfront and ensure you understand the terms before signing any contract.

GUIDE FOR SELECTING AN AGENT OR MANAGER

Step 1: Do Your Research

Start by researching potential agents and managers. Look at their experience, reputation, and the services they offer. You can also seek recommendations from mentors, coaches, or other athletes.

Step 2: Conduct Interviews

Once you have a shortlist of potential agents or managers, conduct interviews to assess their suitability. Use these interviews to gauge their understanding of your vision and their ability to support you in achieving your goals.

Step 3: Review Their Contract

Before signing with an agent or manager, carefully review their contract. Ensure you understand the services they will provide, their fees, and the duration of the contract. You may also want to seek legal advice to ensure you're protecting your interests.

Step 4: Check References

Check references from previous or current clients. This can give you insights into the agent's or manager's reliability, effectiveness, and the quality of their services.

Step 5: Make an Informed Decision

Once you've gathered all the necessary information, you're in a position to make an informed decision. Choose an agent or manager who aligns with your values, supports your vision, and can effectively manage your NIL interests.

ESSENTIAL LEGAL CONSIDERATIONS: UNDERSTANDING NIL CONTRACTS

As you begin to monetize your NIL, you will likely enter into various contracts with sponsors, advertisers, and possibly agents or managers. Understanding the legal implications of these contracts is essential for protecting your interests and maximizing your NIL value.

A contract is a legally binding agreement between two or more parties. In the context of NIL, contracts often outline the details of endorsement deals, sponsorship arrangements, or representation agreements. These contracts can be complex, and understanding them can be challenging.

Here are some essential elements and considerations when reviewing NIL contracts:

1. PARTIES INVOLVED

This refers to who is involved in the contract. It's essential to know the entities you are legally bound to upon signing the agreement.

2. SCOPE OF WORK

The scope of work outlines what you are expected to do under the contract. It could involve appearing in advertisements, promoting products on social media, or attending events. Ensure that the scope of work is clearly defined and that you are comfortable with what's expected of you.

3. COMPENSATION

The contract should clearly state how much you will be paid, when you will be paid, and how payment will be made. It should also outline if there are any conditions to be met for payment.

4. TERM AND TERMINATION

The term refers to how long the contract lasts, while termination conditions outline how and when the contract can be ended by either party. Make sure these terms are clear, and that you are comfortable with the duration and termination provisions of the contract.

5. EXCLUSIVITY

Exclusivity clauses restrict you from entering into similar agreements with other companies. Ensure you understand the extent of these clauses, as they could limit your ability to maximize your NIL earnings.

6. INTELLECTUAL PROPERTY RIGHTS

These provisions outline who owns the rights to any content produced during the agreement. This could significantly impact your ability to use this content in the future.

7. CONFIDENTIALITY AND NON-DISPARAGEMENT

Confidentiality clauses restrict your ability to share certain information about the contract or the company. Non-disparagement clauses restrict you from making negative comments about the company. It's important to understand these provisions, as violating them can have significant legal consequences.

8. INDEMNIFICATION

Indemnification clauses outline who is responsible if legal issues arise from the contract. It's essential to understand these clauses, as they could leave you responsible for substantial legal costs.

Considering these factors when reviewing NIL contracts can help you navigate legal implications and protect your interests. However, due to the complexity of contract law, it is highly recommended to consult with a legal professional before signing any contract.

RISK MANAGEMENT: PROTECTING YOUR NIL VALUE

In the realm of NIL, there are various risks that could potentially harm your brand, limit your earning potential, or even jeopardize your athletic eligibility. Hence, risk management is a critical aspect of protecting your NIL value.

Risk management involves identifying potential risks, assessing their impact, and taking steps to mitigate them. Here are some strategies for managing risks associated with your NIL.

1. MAINTAINING ATHLETIC ELIGIBILITY

One of the primary risks for college athletes pursuing NIL opportunities is the potential loss of athletic eligibility due to non-compliance with NCAA rules or university policies. Ensure you understand these rules and policies, and consult with compliance officers or legal advisors as necessary.

2. PROTECTING YOUR BRAND

Your brand is a key asset in your NIL endeavors, and damage to your brand could have a significant impact on your NIL value. Protect your brand by aligning with companies that reflect your values, managing your online presence responsibly, and maintaining your performance on and off the field.

3. MANAGING INTELLECTUAL PROPERTY RIGHTS

Intellectual property rights can have significant implications for your NIL value. Ensuring that you retain the rights to your image, likeness, and any content you produce is crucial. Consult with a legal professional to understand your rights and to ensure they are protected in any contract you enter into.

4. BALANCING COMMITMENTS

NIL activities can be time-consuming and potentially distracting. It's important to balance your NIL commitments with your academic and athletic responsibilities. Failure to do so could harm your academic performance or athletic career, which in turn, could affect your NIL value.

5. ENSURING FAIR COMPENSATION

Make sure you are being fairly compensated for the use of your NIL. This might involve researching market rates, negotiating contracts, and potentially engaging an agent or manager to advocate on your behalf.

6. MITIGATING LEGAL RISKS

There are numerous legal risks associated with NIL activities, including breach of contract, defamation, and violation of intellectual property rights. Engage a legal professional to help you understand these risks and take steps to mitigate them.

7. PLANNING FOR FINANCIAL IMPLICATIONS

NIL activities can have significant financial implications, including tax liabilities and potential impacts on financial aid. Work with a financial advisor to understand these implications and to plan accordingly.

HEALTH MANAGEMENT: PRESERVING YOUR ATHLETIC PERFORMANCE FOR NIL OPPORTUNITIES

As an athlete, your physical health is an essential asset. After all, your athletic performance is one of the key reasons why companies are interested in partnering with you for NIL opportunities. Therefore, effectively managing your health is crucial to maintain and enhance your athletic performance, and by extension, your NIL value.

Physical health management for athletes is multifaceted. It goes beyond simply avoiding injury. It involves proactive strategies to optimize your health and performance, including nutrition, exercise, rest, and mental health.

NUTRITION

Proper nutrition fuels your body for training and recovery. It can help you perform at your peak, prevent injury, and speed up recovery after workouts. Consider working with a sports nutritionist to create a personalized meal plan that aligns with your training schedule and nutritional needs.

A balanced diet for athletes typically includes a mix of macronutrients—proteins, carbohydrates, and fats—and micronutrients—vitamins and minerals. Hydration is equally crucial as water plays a critical role in nearly every bodily function, including temperature regulation, nutrient transportation, and muscle function.

EXERCISE AND TRAINING

Your exercise and training routine is integral to your athletic performance. However, it's crucial to ensure that your routine is balanced and sustainable to prevent overuse injuries. Work with your coaches and trainers to develop a program that challenges you, but also allows for adequate rest and recovery.

In addition to sport-specific training, consider incorporating cross-training activities to work for different muscle groups and prevent repetitive stress on specific muscles. Flexibility and strength training can also help prevent injuries and enhance your performance.

REST AND RECOVERY

Rest and recovery are often overlooked aspects of athletic performance. However, they are critical for muscle repair, energy replenishment, and mental rejuvenation. Without adequate rest, your performance may suffer, and your risk of injury may increase.

Aim for seven to nine hours of sleep per night. Besides sleep, incorporate active recovery strategies into your routine, such as light physical activity on rest days, stretching, and mobility exercises.

REGULAR HEALTH CHECK-UPS

Regular health check-ups allow for early detection of potential health issues that could affect your performance. These might include physical exams, vision tests, and other relevant screenings.

By prioritizing your health, you not only safeguard your athletic performance but also ensure you're in the best position to maximize your NIL opportunities. Remember, your ability to perform as an athlete is intrinsically tied to your

NIL value. Thus, a commitment to comprehensive health management isn't just beneficial for your athletic career; it's a strategic move for your entrepreneurial endeavors as well.

In the next chapter, we'll delve into how to navigate NIL opportunities while maintaining your academic commitments, ensuring you're not just a successful athlete and entrepreneur, but also a thriving student. Are you ready?

FOUR

NAVIGATING THE NIL LANDSCAPE

The rise of the digital era has revolutionized the land-scape of sports and entertainment. Today, athletes have the opportunity to engage with fans and followers far beyond the field or court, thanks to the proliferation of social media platforms and digital content. As you already know now, the NIL legislation has amplified these opportunities, allowing athletes to leverage their unique brand to establish a presence in the entertainment industry while still actively participating in sports. Understanding the intersection of sports, entertainment, and NIL is crucial for athletes look-ing to navigate this dynamic landscape effectively.

SPORTS AND ENTERTAINMENT: A CONVERGENCE

The line between sports and entertainment has been blurring for decades. Athletes are no longer seen solely as competitors; they are celebrities, influencers, and brands unto themselves. This convergence has opened up a plethora of opportunities for athletes to extend their reach beyond the game. They appear in movies, host TV shows, launch music careers, and become influencers, all while maintaining their athletic careers.

This trend has been accelerated by the advent of digital platforms. Social media platforms like Instagram, X (formerly Twitter), and TikTok have provided athletes with direct channels to engage with fans and followers while streaming platforms have opened up opportunities for athletes to produce and distribute their content.

NAVIGATING THE LANDSCAPE

Remember, the most successful athletes in the NIL landscape are those who are authentic, strategic, and consistent in their branding and activities. By understanding the intersection of sports, entertainment, and NIL, and by applying these strategies, you can effectively navigate this exciting landscape and maximize your opportunities.

Nonetheless, you have to explore how to develop a robust NIL strategy and turn these principles into action. This entails identifying economic opportunities, assessing them critically, and taking steps to manage potential risks.

IDENTIFYING ECONOMIC OPPORTUNITIES

The landscape of NIL has created a sea of economic opportunities for student athletes. In this section, we'll discuss a range of potential economic opportunities associated with NIL and provide practical guidance on how to identify those that might be the best fit for you.

Product Endorsements

Product endorsements are one of the most lucrative opportunities for athletes in the NIL era. This involves promoting a company's products or services in exchange for payment. Successful endorsements are often those that align with an athlete's brand, sport, lifestyle, or personal interests. For example, a collegiate basketball player might endorse a popular shoe brand, while a track star might align with a fitness supplement company.

Identifying endorsement opportunities requires research into potential brands for alignment with your values and marketability. It also requires understanding the company's target market, product range, and marketing strategies. Establishing a genuine connection with the brand can boost the endorsement's credibility and effectiveness.

Sponsored Social Media Content

With the rise of digital platforms, social media has become a powerful tool for monetizing NIL. Athletes can collaborate with brands to create sponsored content for their followers. These collaborations could take the form of posts, videos, stories, or live events that highlight a brand or product.

To identify potential social media sponsorship opportunities, athletes should analyze their follower demographics, engagement rates, and content performance. Look for brands that your followers would find interesting or relevant. Maintaining authenticity is crucial, as followers are quick to notice insincere endorsements.

Personal Merchandise Lines

Creating a personal merchandise line can be another avenue for generating income. This could include clothing, accessories, training gear, or any product that resonates with your brand and fan base.

When considering this opportunity, reflect on your brand attributes, follower demographics, and market demand. Understanding your fans' interests can guide the development of merchandise they're likely to purchase.

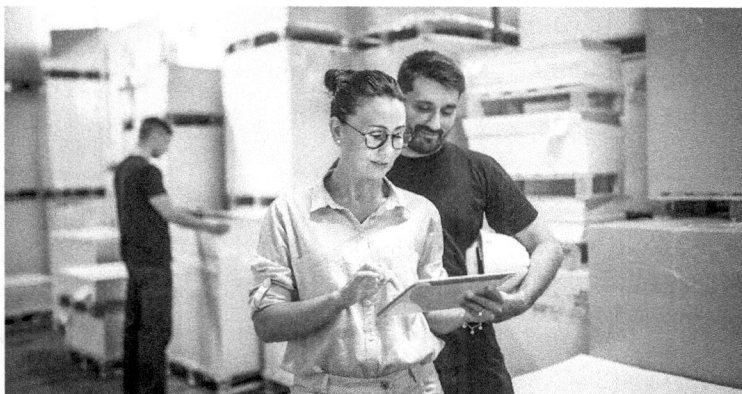

Personal Appearances and Speaking Engagements
Personal appearances at events, sports camps, autograph signings, or speaking engagements can also generate revenue. They provide a platform to share experiences, engage with fans, and enhance your personal brand.

To find such opportunities, build a strong network with organizations, event managers, and schools that could benefit from your presence. Also, focus on improving public speaking and interpersonal skills, which are key to success in this area.

DIGITAL PRODUCTS AND ONLINE PLATFORMS

The digital world offers myriad opportunities for monetizing NIL. Athletes could create and sell digital products such as eBooks, online courses, or training programs. Alternatively, athletes could build online platforms, such as a subscription-based website or app, that offer exclusive content or access.

To identify these opportunities, consider your unique skills, knowledge, or experiences that could be valuable to others. Market research is critical to understand the potential demand and competition for your digital product or platform.

INVESTMENTS AND BUSINESS VENTURES

Lastly, athletes could use their NIL earnings to invest in businesses, startups, or real estate. Such investments could provide additional income and potentially grow in value over time. However, they require careful research, financial literacy, and often the advice of a financial advisor.

Identifying the right investment or business venture involves understanding your financial goals, risk tolerance, and market trends. It's crucial to conduct due diligence, analyzing the potential return and risk associated with each opportunity.

ASSESSING OPPORTUNITIES CRITICALLY

The advent of NIL rights has flung wide the doors of opportunity for student athletes. Yet, amid the flurry of contracts and endorsement offers, it's essential not to lose sight of one crucial skill—the ability to assess opportunities critically. Not every opportunity will align with your long-term objectives or personal brand. Making decisions hastily or without due consideration could lead to pitfalls that might be difficult to recover from.

When assessing an opportunity, start by examining its specifics thoroughly. Understand the financial implications and commitments involved. What are the immediate gains? Is there potential for long-term benefits? Scrutinize the fine print of contracts and agreements. Are there conditions or clauses that might limit other opportunities or infringe on your rights? If the terms are complex, consider consulting with a lawyer or an agent experienced in NIL contracts.

Next, consider how well the opportunity aligns with your personal brand. Every endorsement or contract you sign will reflect back on you. If a product or company doesn't fit with the image you've cultivated, endorsing it might dilute your brand and confuse your audience. A misalignment might even risk alienating your fans, leading to a loss of credibility and possibly harming your career in the long term.

Beyond brand alignment, think about your core values and principles. Every decision you make should uphold these foundational elements. If an endorsement opportunity forces you to compromise on your beliefs or operate outside your comfort zone, it may lead to dissatisfaction and regret, no matter the financial gains.

Think about the opportunity in terms of your career trajectory. Does it offer opportunities for professional growth or to develop new skills? Can it help expand your network or provide valuable exposure in your field? Remember, some opportunities that may not offer substantial financial benefits immediately could still be incredibly valuable for your future career growth.

Time commitment is another crucial factor to consider. Will this opportunity interfere with your primary responsibilities as a student and an athlete? Striking a balance between your commitments is vital. Overstretching yourself could affect your performance, both on the field and in the classroom.

Finally, don't forget the power of a second opinion. Seek advice from trusted mentors, coaches, or professionals in the industry. These individuals have a wealth of experience and can provide insights that you might have overlooked.

They can guide you toward making informed decisions that align with your personal and professional goals.

Assessing opportunities critically is not a skill you develop overnight. It requires patience, due diligence, and an in-depth understanding of your personal brand and career aspirations. However, honing this ability will pay dividends in the long run, helping you navigate the complex landscape of NIL and truly unlock your potential.

MANAGING POTENTIAL RISKS

As student-athletes venture into the monetization of their NIL, they must also acknowledge and effectively manage the potential risks involved. From contractual pitfalls to damage to personal brand and the possibility of regulatory violations, the NIL landscape is fraught with challenges. This section will discuss some of the key risks student athletes may encounter and provide strategies to manage them effectively.

UNDERSTANDING CONTRACTUAL OBLIGATIONS

A fundamental risk associated with NIL opportunities stems from contractual agreements. Contracts can be intricate, laden with legal jargon and fine print that may hide unfavorable clauses. Some of these clauses may have lasting implications, such as exclusivity terms that prevent athletes from engaging with other brands, or clauses that impose penalties for failing to meet certain conditions.

As mentioned repeatedly, given its high level of importance, athletes must strive to understand their contractual obligations fully. It is beneficial to hire a competent lawyer or agent who can explain the contract's implications. They can also negotiate on the athlete's behalf to ensure terms are as favorable as possible. Furthermore, athletes should ensure they're comfortable with all contract terms before signing, as contracts can be binding and difficult to terminate without legal ramifications.

PRESERVING PERSONAL BRAND

Another significant risk for student athletes entering the NIL space is damage to their personal brand. This could happen if an athlete endorses a controversial product, posts inappropriate content, or behaves in a way that fans perceive negatively.

To mitigate this risk, athletes should establish a clear personal brand identity, complete with defined values and standards. By understanding what their brand stands for, they can make decisions that align with this identity. They should also conduct thorough research before aligning with brands or individuals, ensuring that these entities share similar values. Maintaining consistency in behavior and communication is key to preserving brand identity.

REGULATORY COMPLIANCE

Ensuring regulatory compliance is another critical risk management aspect. Violating NCAA rules, for example, could lead to severe consequences such as disqualification from collegiate sports. Additionally, student athletes must also be aware of state and federal laws related to marketing, copyright, and taxes.

To manage regulatory risks, athletes should familiarize themselves with applicable regulations and stay updated on any changes. Engaging a knowledgeable agent or legal counsel can help in this area. Consulting with a financial advisor can also ensure athletes understand and meet their other obligations.

TIME MANAGEMENT CHALLENGES

Time management can pose a significant challenge as athletes juggle their responsibilities in sports, academics, and now, NIL-related commitments. Mismanagement could lead to poor academic performance, decreased athletic performance, or breach of NIL contract obligations.

Athletes can mitigate this risk by developing robust time management skills. Prioritizing tasks, setting a realistic schedule, and allowing for sufficient rest and relaxation are all crucial. Additionally, athletes should be mindful of their limits and not overcommit to NIL opportunities.

FINANCIAL RISKS

Finally, athletes should be cognizant of financial risks. Mismanaging NIL earnings, falling for fraudulent schemes, or investing in unsuccessful ventures can lead to financial loss.

To manage financial risks, athletes should prioritize financial literacy. This includes understanding how to budget, save, invest, and pay taxes. Athletes should also work with trustworthy financial advisors and be wary of too-good-to-be-true investment opportunities.

DEALING WITH CONTRACT DISPUTES

Contract disputes can be another source of legal challenges in the NIL arena. If a company or individual alleges that you have not met the terms of your agreement, or if you believe that the other party has breached your contract, this could lead to a dispute.

Firstly, always consult your legal counsel. They can help you understand the implications of the dispute and guide you on the best course of action. Secondly, refer back to your contract. The contract should outline the process for dealing with disputes, which may include negotiation, mediation, or arbitration before resorting to litigation.

ADDRESSING UNAUTHORIZED USE OF YOUR NIL

If a third party uses your Name, Image, or Likeness without your permission, you may need to take legal action to protect your rights. The first step is usually to issue a cease and desist letter, notifying the other party of the infringement and demanding that they stop the unauthorized use. If this doesn't resolve the issue, you may need to consider further legal action, such as filing a lawsuit.

STAYING COMPLIANT WITH REGULATIONS

The legal landscape around NIL is constantly evolving with new legislation, court rulings, and policy changes potentially impacting your rights and responsibilities. Stay informed about changes that could affect you, and consult with your legal counsel to ensure you remain compliant with all relevant regulations.

Legal challenges in the NIL landscape can seem daunting, but with a strong understanding of your rights and responsibilities, and with the support of professional legal advice, you can navigate these challenges effectively and continue to maximize your NIL opportunities.

STAYING AHEAD: KEEPING ABREAST
OF NIL TRENDS AND CHANGES

The landscape of NIL rights is ever-evolving. Changes in laws, NCAA regulations, and social and cultural trends can all impact the ways in which athletes can capitalize on their NIL. Staying ahead of these changes is key to maintaining and growing your NIL value.

MONITORING LEGAL AND REGULATORY CHANGES

Legal and regulatory changes can have significant impacts on your NIL rights. Stay informed about developments in state and federal NIL legislation, changes to NCAA rules, and relevant court cases. This will help you understand your current rights and responsibilities, anticipate potential changes, and adapt your strategy accordingly. More about this in Chapter Ten.

UNDERSTANDING MARKET TRENDS

Changes in consumer behavior, media consumption, and the popularity of different sports or events can all affect the demand for your NIL. Monitor trends in your sport and the broader market to identify new opportunities and anticipate potential challenges.

EMBRACING TECHNOLOGICAL INNOVATIONS

Advances in technology continually create new platforms and methods for athletes to connect with fans and monetize their NIL. From social media platforms to virtual and augmented reality, these innovations offer exciting new ways to engage with fans and generate revenue. Stay abreast of technological trends and be open to exploring these new avenues.

LEARNING FROM OTHER ATHLETES

Keep an eye on how other athletes, particularly those in your sport, are utilizing their NIL. Their successes (and failures) can provide valuable lessons and inspiration for your own NIL strategy.

NETWORKING AND PROFESSIONAL DEVELOPMENT

Regularly engage with industry professionals, such as sports marketers, agents, and lawyers. These individuals can provide insights into current trends and changes and can offer advice tailored to your specific situation. Consider attending industry events, joining professional associations, and enrolling in relevant courses or workshops to further your knowledge and connections.

ADJUSTING YOUR STRATEGY

Staying ahead of trends and changes isn't just about awareness; it's about action. Regularly reassess and adjust your NIL strategy in response to the changes you observe. This could mean pivoting your focus, renegotiating contracts, or investing in new areas.

FIVE

EXPLORING SOCIAL MEDIA AND MULTIMEDIA IMPLEMENTATION

I n the era of NIL rights, an athlete's online presence has never been more important. Social media platforms are not just for communication anymore. They have become a crucial venue for building your brand, engaging with fans, and capitalizing on your NIL. But with great potential also comes great responsibility. Effectively managing your social media presence is a critical skill for every athlete navigating the NIL landscape.

UNDERSTANDING DIFFERENT PLATFORMS

Different social media platforms cater to different demographics and serve different purposes. Understanding these differences is the first step to optimizing your online presence.

1. **Facebook**: Facebook's extensive user base makes it a powerful tool for reaching a broad audience. It's ideal for longer posts, event announcements, and direct fan engagement through comments and messages.

2. **X (formerly Twitter)**: X is all about real-time communication. It's great for sharing quick updates, commenting on live events, and engaging in conversations.

3. **Instagram**: Instagram is highly visual, making it perfect for sharing photos and short videos. It's particularly popular among younger demographics.

4. **LinkedIn**: LinkedIn is a professional networking platform. It's less about fan engagement and more about building professional connections and showcasing your off-the-field achievements and aspirations.

5. **TikTok**: TikTok is all about short, creative videos. It's massively popular among Gen Z and is a great platform for showing off your personality and creativity.

Consider your target audience, your content strategy, and your strengths when deciding which platforms to focus on.

CRAFTING YOUR SOCIAL MEDIA PERSONA

Your social media persona should be an authentic reflection of who you are, but it's also a powerful tool for shaping your public image. Think about what you want to be known for, both as an athlete and as a person. Are you all about dedication and hard work? Are you a fun-loving team player? Or are you a passionate advocate for a cause? Incorporate these themes into your posts to build a consistent and engaging persona.

ENGAGING WITH YOUR AUDIENCE

Engaging with your audience is not just about sharing content; it's also about interaction. Respond to comments, ask questions, and show appreciation for your fans. This can help build a loyal and engaged fanbase.

MANAGING RISKS

With the benefits of social media come risks. A poorly thought-out post can damage your reputation, while an innocent mistake can lead to accusations of copyright infringement or other legal issues. Always think before you post, respect others' rights, and consider the potential impact on your public image.

LEVERAGING YOUR SOCIAL MEDIA FOR NIL OPPORTUNITIES

Once you have a strong online presence and an engaged audience, you can start leveraging your social media for NIL opportunities. This could include sponsored posts, brand partnerships, crowdfunding campaigns, or even launching your products or services.

THE IMPORTANCE OF HAVING A WEBSITE

Although social media platforms allow you to connect with fans and potential sponsors on a large scale, a personal website offers an exclusive platform that you control completely. It grants you the freedom to tailor the content and design to fit your brand.

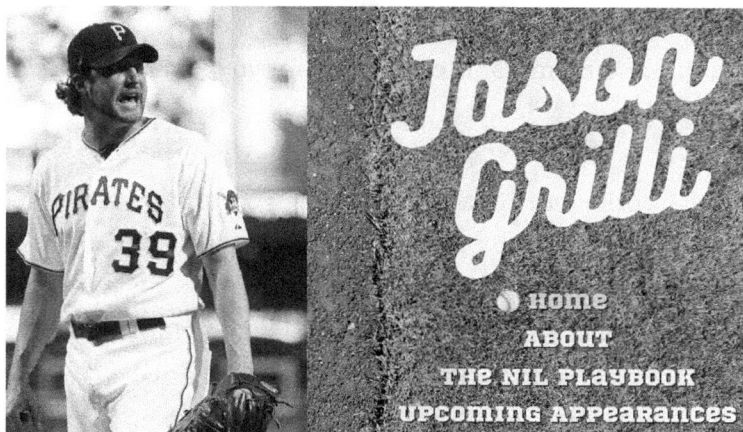

A PERSONAL TOUCH

One of the key benefits of a personal website is the opportunity to provide a deeper look into who you are, both as an athlete and as an individual. This can range from sharing your personal journey, goals, and values, to featuring behind-the-scenes content that may not fit into the snippets typically shared on social media. It's your space to express yourself and differentiate yourself from other athletes.

ENDLESS CUSTOMIZATION OPPORTUNITIES

In contrast to the rigid templates of social media, a website gives you the freedom to experiment with designs and formats that best reflect your brand. You can choose colors, fonts, layouts, and multimedia elements that align with your brand image. This flexibility allows you to create a unique and memorable experience for your visitors.

CONSOLIDATING YOUR ONLINE PRESENCE

Your website can act as a hub for all your online activities. It can host links to your social media profiles, showcase your photo and video galleries, display upcoming events or competitions, and even include a blog for more extensive reflections or stories. This consolidation can make it easier for fans, media, and potential sponsors to find all the information about you in one place.

CONTROL OVER MONETIZATION

Your website is a platform where you have direct control over monetization strategies. From selling merchandise and offering exclusive content to fan clubs to hosting advertisements and gaining sponsorships, a website can become a significant source of revenue, fully aligned with your NIL rights.

LONG-TERM RELEVANCE

While the popularity of social media platforms can rise and fall, a personal website remains a stable presence. As you progress through your career and beyond, your website can evolve and grow with you, maintaining a constant connection with your fans and followers.

At the conclusion of this chapter, it's clear that establishing a strong online presence through both social media and a personal website is vital in this era of NIL. By understanding and leveraging various platforms, crafting an engaging persona, interacting with your audience, managing risks, and utilizing these digital avenues for NIL opportunities, you can greatly amplify your brand.

Remember, in the realm of NIL, you're not just an athlete; you're a brand—an individual with unique stories, achievements, and potential. Just as in athletics, success in managing your digital presence and leveraging NIL opportunities requires strategy, effort, and dedication. The integration of social media management and your website, together, can unlock the expansive potential of your NIL.

In the upcoming sections, we will delve deeper into maximizing this potential, bringing you to even greater heights in the NIL landscape. Are you ready to venture further?

MAXIMIZING THE VALUE OF NIL BY DEEPENING UNDERSTANDING OF MULTIMEDIA INTEGRATION

Beyond the textual and photographic content traditionally shared on social media, there's a whole universe of multimedia options that can significantly enhance your online persona and fan engagement. Embracing these tools not only boosts your content's appeal but also opens up new avenues for NIL monetization.

1. **Video Content**: As we just showed you, platforms like Instagram, TikTok, and YouTube have popularized video content. Short clips can showcase your training regimen, game highlights, or even day-to-day life, offering fans an intimate glimpse into your world. Longer-form content, such as personal vlogs or in-depth interviews, can be a powerful tool to share your journey and aspirations.

2. **Live Streaming**: With features like Instagram Live, Facebook Live, and Twitch, you can interact with fans in real time. This could include Q&A sessions, live game reactions, or just casual chats. Live streams foster a sense of community and real-time engagement, creating a more personal connection with your fans.

3. **Podcasts**: For athletes with a lot to say, podcasts offer a platform to delve into topics you're passionate about. Whether it's discussing game strategies, sharing personal experiences, or advocating for causes close to your heart, podcasts allow you to engage your audience in a more in-depth conversation.

4. **Augmented Reality (AR) and Virtual Reality (VR)**: Snapchat lenses, Instagram filters, or more immersive VR experiences offer interactive ways to engage your followers. These technologies can provide unique fan experiences, such as virtual meet-and-greets or virtual tours of your training grounds.

5. **Interactive Posts**: Platforms like Instagram and Facebook offer options for polls, quizzes, or other interactive posts. These not only increase engagement but also provide valuable insights into your fans' preferences and opinions.

Each multimedia tool offers unique benefits and considerations. While videos might require more planning and editing, podcasts offer a less visually focused, more conversational way to connect. AR and VR can create unforgettable fan experiences but might require more technical knowledge or resources. Interactive posts are simple to implement and can provide instant engagement.

By understanding the strengths and requirements of each multimedia format, which we will soon discuss in more detail, you can choose the tools that best align with your personal brand, content strategy, and available resources. A smart multimedia strategy not only elevates your social media presence but also creates richer, more engaging fan interactions, thereby multiplying NIL opportunities.

ENGAGEMENT AND PERSONAL CONNECTION

Engagement and personal connection are critical because they represent your ability to connect with fans on a deeper level, beyond just the surface. In today's social media-driven world, people crave genuine connections with the individuals they admire. Your fans don't just want to watch you on the field or court; they want to feel connected to you in some way. That connection is what drives engagement and ultimately determines the value of your NIL.

Building personal connections is a two-way street. It's not just about posting content online and waiting for likes and comments; it's about engaging with fans, responding to their comments, and showing them that you value their support. This can be done through regular interaction on social media, hosting live Q&A sessions, sharing behind-the-scenes content, or even sending personalized messages to fans. It's about showing up and being present, not just as an athlete, but as a person.

But, remember to remain authentic in your interactions. Authenticity is key to building lasting relationships with fans. Be true to your voice, your values, and your story. Share your struggles, your triumphs, and your daily life as an athlete and an entrepreneur. Let your fans see the person behind the athlete, the individual with dreams, aspirations, and challenges just like them. This personal connection will not only increase the value of your NIL but also build a strong foundation for your entrepreneurial journey.

After you've cultivated a strong personal connection with your audience, it's time to explore the direct monetization opportunities of your NIL.

DIRECT MONETIZATION OPPORTUNITIES

Direct monetization involves converting your engagement and personal connections into income streams. There are several ways you can monetize your NIL.

Sponsored Posts

Sponsored posts are a common way athletes monetize their social media presence. Companies pay athletes to promote their products or services on their social media accounts. The value of a sponsored post will depend on your follower count, engagement rate, and the demographic of your audience.

But it's not just about promoting any product that comes your way. To maintain your authenticity and trust with your audience, it's important to only partner with brands that align with your values and your brand. Your audience trusts you and your recommendations; therefore, the products you endorse should be ones that you genuinely believe in and use.

Affiliate Marketing

Affiliate marketing is another way you can generate income from your NIL. With affiliate marketing, you promote a company's product or service, and in return, you earn a commission from every sale made through your unique affiliate link. It's an effective way to monetize your social media presence, especially if you have a large and engaged following.

Like sponsored posts, make sure to only affiliate with brands and products you trust and personally vouch for. Your reputation is at stake.

Ad Revenue from YouTube Videos

If you're comfortable in front of a camera, creating YouTube videos can be another lucrative way to monetize your NIL. YouTube allows content creators to earn money from ads displayed on their videos. You can create a variety of content, from training videos, and game reviews, to day-in-the-life vlogs. The key is to create content that your audience enjoys and finds value in. By regularly posting quality content and engaging with your audience, you can build a large and dedicated YouTube following, increasing your ad revenue.

Again, authenticity is key. Your videos should align with your personal brand and values, and be something you enjoy creating. As you grow your following, you might also attract sponsorship opportunities directly related to your YouTube content.

DATA ANALYTICS

In the digital age, data has become the cornerstone of effective decision-making. Analytics offer you insights about your fans and followers: Who they are, Where they are from, What they like, and How they engage with your content. All of this data can inform your content strategy, brand positioning, and monetization efforts, allowing you to make data-driven decisions that optimize the value of your NIL.

Understanding Your Audience

Understanding your audience is critical in maximizing the value of your NIL. Social media platforms and websites provide a wealth of data about your followers, including their age, gender, location, and interests. By analyzing this data, you can tailor your content to appeal to your audience, thus increasing engagement.

For example, if a significant portion of your followers are young athletes looking to improve their performance, you might create content that focuses on training techniques, nutrition advice, or mental conditioning. Similarly, if your followers are interested in entrepreneurship, you might share your journey as an athlete-turned-entrepreneur, discussing the challenges you've faced and the lessons you've learned.

Informing Your Content Strategy

Data analytics can also inform your content strategy. By monitoring the performance of your posts (likes, comments, shares, views, etc.), you can identify what type of content resonates most with your audience. This understanding allows you to focus your energy on creating more of the content that your audience loves, increasing engagement, which increases the value of your NIL.

Moreover, you can also identify the best times to post on different platforms to maximize visibility and engagement. Each social media platform has peak usage times which can be leveraged to get your content in front of as many eyes as possible.

Monetization Efforts

Finally, data analytics can inform your monetization efforts. By understanding your audience's demographics and interests, you can identify potential brand partnerships that would be relevant and appealing to your followers. This increases the likelihood that your audience will engage with sponsored content or purchase products through your affiliate links, thereby increasing your income.

Maximizing Live Streaming Opportunities

Live streaming is a powerful tool for maximizing the value of your NIL. It offers a unique way for athletes to engage with their fans in real time, providing a sense of immediacy and intimacy that static posts or pre-recorded videos can't replicate. Moreover, live streaming also presents several monetization opportunities.

Gameplay

For athletes who also enjoy video games, streaming your gameplay can be a lucrative opportunity. Platforms like Twitch allow gamers to earn income through subscriptions, donations, and ad revenue. Additionally, if you're particularly skilled at a game, you might attract sponsorships from gaming companies.

But even if you're not a gamer, you can still leverage live streaming in training sessions or exhibition matches. This gives your fans a chance to see you in action outside of the official games, which can be both entertaining and informative.

Personal Q&A Sessions

Hosting live Q&A sessions is another great way to engage with your audience. These sessions allow your fans to interact with you directly, ask questions, and learn more about you. This not only builds a deeper connection between you and your fans but also offers insights into your fans' interests, which you can use to inform your content strategy.

You can monetize these sessions in several ways. For example, you might have a virtual "tip jar" where fans can donate money, or you can host paid Q&A sessions where fans purchase tickets to participate.

MORE MONETIZATION OPPORTUNITIES

With the tips above, even more monetization opportunities may arise. For example, live streams can also offer "Super Chat" features where viewers can donate money directly during the stream for their messages to be highlighted and read out loud. Platforms like Twitch also offer "bits" or "cheers," a form of virtual currency that viewers can purchase and use to tip or support streamers.

On top of these, brands may be willing to sponsor your live streams. This could involve promoting their products during the stream, using their equipment, or even wearing their clothing. As with all sponsored content, however, transparency is key. It's important to disclose to your viewers any sponsorships to maintain trust and abide by FTC guidelines.

PODCASTING

Podcasting offers a platform to share long-form content, delve into complex topics, and engage in in-depth conversations. You could start a podcast focused on sports, entrepreneurship, or the intersection of the two. Share your personal experiences, interview other athletes or entrepreneurs, or provide advice to aspiring athletes or business owners.

Monetizing your podcast can come in various forms.

Sponsorships and advertising are the most common, with businesses paying to have their products or services mentioned during your podcast. Additionally, affiliate marketing can be a great way to generate income. You could recommend products or services and include your unique affiliate link in your podcast description.

You could also create a premium subscription model, where listeners pay for additional content, early access to episodes, or bonus material. Websites such as Patreon make it easy to set up and manage such a service.

VLOGGING

Vlogging, on the other hand, provides a visual and more personal insight into your life. Whether it's a day in the life of an athlete, behind the scenes at a game, or a peek into your entrepreneurial ventures, vlogging allows your audience to connect with you on a deeper level.

Monetizing your vlog can be similar to a podcast. Advertising, sponsorships, and affiliate marketing are all viable options. Ad revenue through YouTube is a popular method of income, as is sponsored content where companies pay you to feature their products in your vlog.

In both podcasting and vlogging, consistency and authenticity are key. Regularly publishing content and being genuine in your approach will help grow your audience and increase your earning potential.

MERCHANDISING YOUR NIL

Merchandising is another potent avenue for monetizing your NIL. This involves creating and selling products that showcase your NIL, like apparel, collectibles, and more.

Apparel

Apparel is a popular choice for many athletes. This can include items such as T-shirts, hoodies, hats, and even athletic wear, all branded with your name, image, or a logo that represents you. Apparel allows your fans to show their support in a tangible way and provides you with a steady stream of income.

When creating apparel, ensure the products are high quality and reflect your brand. Your merchandise should be something you're proud to sell and something your fans will be proud to wear.

Collectibles

Collectibles are another way to monetize your NIL. This can include items like autographed memorabilia, limited edition artwork, or even collectible cards.

Creating limited edition products can create a sense of exclusivity, making the items more desirable to fans. Plus, collectibles can increase in value over time, making them an investment for your fans.

More NIL Merchandise

The options for merchandising your NIL are limited only by your creativity. Depending on your brand and your fans, you might consider creating other items like books, home goods, or even digital products like online courses or ebooks.

Merchandising your NIL not only provides an additional income stream but also strengthens your brand and deepens your connection with fans. Every piece of merchandise is a form of advertising, expanding the reach of your NIL.

CREATING A PREMIUM FAN CLUB

A Premium Fan Club takes your engagement with fans to another level. This is a group of your most loyal and enthusiastic supporters who are willing to pay a premium to get exclusive access to content, experiences, and merchandise that aren't available to the general public.

Exclusive Content

Exclusive content is the main draw for most Premium Fan Clubs. This could be anything from behind-the-scenes footage, personal blogs, or early access to your vlogs and podcasts. You could also offer content that dives deeper into your life and thoughts. For example, you could have a series where you discuss your thoughts on recent games, delve into your training routines, or share the lessons you've learned in your entrepreneurial journey.

The key to creating compelling exclusive content is to offer something that fans can't get elsewhere. This adds value to your Premium Fan Club and makes the subscription fee worth it.

Exclusive Experiences

In addition to exclusive content, offering exclusive experiences can be a huge draw for your Premium Fan Club. This could include live Q&A sessions, online meet-and-greets, or even virtual training sessions.

You could also offer real-life experiences, such as VIP tickets to your games, exclusive meet-ups, or even the chance to train with you. Such experiences can make your fans feel closer to you, deepen their connection, and make them feel like they're part of your journey.

Premium Merchandise

Offering premium merchandise is another way to add value to your Premium Fan Club. This could be higher-quality apparel, limited-edition collectibles, or even personalized items. Offering merchandise that's exclusive to your Premium Fan Club makes membership more attractive and can increase the value of your NIL.

A Premium Fan Club can be a lucrative source of income, but it also requires a significant time investment to ensure you're providing enough value to justify the membership fee. Be sure to balance the demands of your Premium Fan Club with your other responsibilities as an athlete and an entrepreneur.

LEVERAGING VIRTUAL AND AUGMENTED REALITY

The realms of VR and AR are becoming increasingly popular and offer innovative ways to monetize your NIL. These technologies offer immersive experiences that can bring fans closer to you, in ways not possible with traditional media.

Virtual Reality Experiences

Virtual reality offers immersive, 3D experiences that can make fans feel like they're right there with you. You could offer VR training sessions, where fans can experience what it's like to train with you. Or you could provide a VR experience of a day in your life, giving fans an intimate look at your routine, training, and downtime.

You could also explore VR games. If you're associated with a particular sport, you could have a VR game that simulates playing with you. Fans could learn techniques, practice skills, and even compete in a virtual world.

Augmented Reality Opportunities

Augmented reality adds digital elements to a live view, often through a smartphone camera. AR offers a different set of opportunities to engage with fans and monetize your NIL.

One possibility is AR merchandise. You could sell virtual goods that fans can display in their homes through an AR app. For example, they could purchase a virtual poster that's only visible through their camera app. AR can also enhance physical merchandise. For example, you could sell apparel or collectibles that, when viewed through an AR app, reveal exclusive content.

You could also create an AR app where fans can take selfies with a digital version of you. Or offer an AR tour of your training facilities or a behind-the-scenes look at your game day. The possibilities with AR are vast and limited only by your creativity.

NIL IN E-SPORTS

E-sports is a rapidly growing industry, with an audience that already rivals traditional sports in terms of size and passion. As an athlete transitioning into entrepreneurship, e-sports presents numerous opportunities to monetize your NIL, particularly if you're a gamer yourself.

Streaming and Sponsorships

As mentioned previously, streaming your gameplay on platforms like Twitch can be a lucrative source of income, especially if you're good at the games you play. Beyond ad revenue and donations, successful e-sports athletes often attract sponsorships from game developers, hardware companies, and other businesses related to the gaming industry.

By wearing their gear, using their equipment, or promoting their products during your streams, you can earn a substantial income from sponsorships. Be sure to align yourself with brands that fit your image and values to ensure authenticity and maintain your credibility with your fans.

Teams and Tournaments

You can further capitalize on your NIL in e-sports by joining a team or participating in tournaments. Top e-sports athletes are often part of professional teams, and these affiliations can boost your visibility and income.

Tournaments, on the other hand, offer prize money for winners, and even if you don't win, simply participating can enhance your reputation and increase your fanbase. Plus, tournaments often attract additional sponsorships and endorsement deals.

Coaching and Courses

If you have a high skill level in a particular game, you might consider offering coaching sessions or creating online courses to teach others how to improve. This not only provides a direct source of income but also positions you as an expert and leader in the e-sports community, which can boost the value of your NIL.

ADVANCED AFFILIATE MARKETING STRATEGIES

While basic affiliate marketing involves promoting a product and earning a commission for each sale made through your unique link, there are advanced strategies you can use to maximize your income from endorsements.

Selective Endorsements

While it might be tempting to endorse as many products as possible to maximize income, being selective with your endorsements can actually lead to higher earnings. By choosing to endorse only products that are highly relevant and valuable to your audience, you maintain your credibility and increase the likelihood that your followers will trust your recommendations and make a purchase.

Product Reviews and Tutorials

Rather than simply mentioning a product or sharing a link, consider creating content that provides a detailed review or shows how to use the product. This adds value for your followers and allows them to see the product in action, which can increase their confidence in the product and their likelihood of purchasing.

Exclusive Discounts

Negotiate with the brands you're endorsing to offer exclusive discounts for your followers. This creates an incentive for your followers to make a purchase and can boost your affiliate income.

Tracking and Optimization

Use tracking links to monitor the performance of your affiliate marketing efforts. This allows you to see which products your followers are most interested in and which type of content leads to the most sales. You can then use this data to refine your strategy and maximize your income.

CROWDFUNDING AND FAN FUNDING

Crowdfunding and fan funding can be effective ways to monetize your NIL while also engaging your fans in your journey. By funding specific projects or objectives, you can provide a tangible return on your fans' investment and potentially boost your brand's value.

Crowdfunding Platforms

Platforms like Kickstarter, Indiegogo, and GoFundMe allow you to raise funds for specific projects or goals. This can be especially effective if you have a large and engaged fanbase willing to support you. Some examples of projects that might be appropriate for crowdfunding include launching a clothing line, organizing a charity event, or funding your training for a major competition.

One of the keys to successful crowdfunding is to offer enticing rewards for different levels of support. This could be merchandise, exclusive content, or even experiences like a personal meet-and-greet. By offering rewards that your fans value, you can incentivize more support and increase the value of your NIL.

Fan Funding Platforms

Fan funding platforms like Patreon allow fans to support you on an ongoing basis, often in exchange for exclusive content or experiences. This can be a more sustainable source of income than project-based crowdfunding, as it provides regular support and allows you to build a closer relationship with your fans.

The key to successful fan funding is to consistently provide value to your supporters. This could be through exclusive content, early access to your products or services, or personal interactions. By regularly engaging your fans and showing appreciation for their support, you can foster a loyal fanbase that is more likely to continue supporting you.

MENTORSHIP PROGRAMS

Mentorship programs allow you to provide guidance and advice to less experienced individuals in your field. This can be a more informal and flexible way to share your knowledge than structured coaching services.

One way to monetize mentorship is by offering a mentorship subscription, where mentees pay a regular fee for ongoing access to your advice and guidance. Alternatively, you could offer specific mentorship packages, like a six-week program for aspiring athletes or entrepreneurs.

Mentorship can be a rewarding way to share your experiences and lessons learned, and it can also enhance your reputation and the value of your NIL.

CONSULTING SERVICES

Your knowledge in your respective sport, along with your entrepreneurial acumen, can be incredibly beneficial to organizations and individuals alike. You might consider offering consulting services related to sports performance, fitness, nutrition, leadership, and teamwork, or any other areas where your expertise lies.

You could consult with sports teams, athletic organizations, or even businesses that want to improve their team dynamics or leadership skills. The scope of your services will depend on your specific skills and experiences but might include advising on training programs, providing feedback on performance, or developing strategies for success.

While consulting can provide a significant income, it can also help establish you as an expert in your field, which can enhance your NIL value. It's important to deliver clear and measurable value to your clients, as their success and satisfaction can lead to more consulting opportunities.

SPEAKING ENGAGEMENTS

Public speaking is another powerful way to monetize your NIL. By sharing your story and insights at conferences, corporate events, or sports seminars, you can inspire others and gain recognition as a thought leader in your field.

There are numerous topics you might speak on, depending on your experiences and interests. You might share stories from your athletic career, lessons learned in your transition to entrepreneurship, or insights into performance, leadership, or resilience.

Speaking engagements not only provide an income but can also raise your profile and extend your reach, potentially attracting more fans, followers, or clients.

When preparing for a speaking engagement, it's crucial to understand your audience and tailor your message to their needs and interests. By delivering an engaging and impactful speech, you can leave a lasting impression and increase the demand for your speaking services.

Here are some tips for effective public speaking:

1. **Know Your Audience**: Understand who you're speaking to and what they're interested in or struggling with. This can help you tailor your

message to their needs and make a deeper connection.

2. **Be Personal**: Share personal stories and experiences to illustrate your points. This can help you build trust and rapport with your audience.

3. **Engage Your Audience**: Encourage questions, invite participation, and use visuals or interactive elements to keep your audience engaged and interested.

4. **Practice**: The more you practice, the more confident and polished you'll be on the day of your speech.

THE ECONOMICS OF CELEBRITY: LESSONS FROM TOP EARNERS

In the world of Name, Image, and Likeness, athletes can glean invaluable insights from studying the financial strategies of top-earning celebrities. These individuals have mastered the art of transforming their public personas into profitable ventures, through a myriad of avenues including product endorsements, personal branding, and strategic investments. To round up this chapter, we dissect the economics of celebrity, distilling lessons that can be applied by student athletes looking to maximize their NIL value.

CAPITALIZING ON INFLUENCE

A major aspect of a celebrity's financial strategy is capitalizing on their influence. A public figure with a large and engaged following presents an attractive opportunity for companies looking to promote their products or services. Successful celebrities understand this and strategically choose partnerships that align with their personal brand, further solidifying their market position and increasing their earning potential.

Lesson: Leverage your NIL for endorsements and partnerships that align with your brand. This will not only provide a source of income but also strengthen your brand image and increase your attractiveness to future sponsors.

DIVERSIFYING REVENUE STREAMS

Top-earning celebrities often have diverse revenue streams. They understand that relying solely on their primary career (acting, singing, playing a sport) can be risky due to the uncertainty and short lifespan of these professions. As such, they diversify their income through avenues like product lines, real estate investments, and ownership stakes in companies.

Lesson: Diversify your revenue streams. This could mean launching your own merchandise line, investing in stocks or real estate, or exploring other business ventures. Diversification can provide financial stability and open up new growth opportunities.

BUILDING AND PROTECTING A PERSONAL BRAND

High-earning celebrities also invest significant time and resources into building and protecting their personal brands. They understand that their brand is their most valuable asset—it influences their appeal to sponsors, their relationship with fans, and their overall market value.

Lesson: Invest in your personal brand. This involves defining your brand values, consistently representing these values in your public activities, and taking steps to protect your brand from reputational harm.

ENGAGING IN STRATEGIC PHILANTHROPY

Many successful celebrities are also known for their philanthropic efforts. While these activities are often driven by a genuine desire to make a positive impact, they also serve a strategic purpose. Philanthropy can enhance a celebrity's public image, strengthen their brand, and even provide tax benefits.

Lesson: Consider engaging in philanthropy. This could mean donating a portion of your NIL earnings to a cause you care about, volunteering your time, or using your platform to raise awareness. Philanthropy can enrich your brand while also making a positive impact in your community.

MAINTAINING FINANCIAL LITERACY

Lastly, successful celebrities understand the importance of financial literacy. They know how to manage their finances, navigate tax implications, and make informed investment decisions. This knowledge enables them to protect their wealth, maximize their earnings, and ensure their long-term financial stability.

Lesson: Prioritize financial literacy. This might involve consulting with a financial advisor, taking courses, or educating yourself through books and other resources. Financial literacy is crucial for managing your NIL earnings effectively and securing your financial future.

SIX

BALANCING NIL WITH YOUR EDUCATION

The balancing act between maximizing your NIL and pursuing an education is one that many student athletes grapple with. As an athlete, you may be presented with substantial opportunities to earn money from your NIL, creating a real temptation to focus more on these immediate economic gains than on your long-term educational goals. However, it is crucial to understand that education plays a significant role in enhancing your NIL. Let's delve into this complex relationship to help you navigate it efficiently.

THE ROLE OF EDUCATION IN ENHANCING NIL

The value of an athlete's Name, Image, and Likeness goes beyond the prowess they exhibit on the field, the court, the track, or the pool. Yes, athletic performance is a substantial part of your value as an athlete, but other aspects play a crucial role as well. An essential part of that equation is your education.

Your intellectual acumen, your ability to communicate effectively, and your understanding of societal issues, which are all fostered by your educational background, are elements that contribute significantly to your overall NIL. People connect not only with the athlete you are but also with the person you are—your thoughts, your opinions, your values—and education plays a pivotal role in shaping these.

Brands seek athletes who resonate with their target market. This resonance is often established through shared values and relatable narratives. Being knowledgeable and articulate, therefore, makes you an attractive partner for brands. In this way, education is an invaluable tool that allows you to broaden your appeal, expand your audience base, and enhance your NIL.

Education also offers a framework for understanding the business and legal aspects of your NIL. The world of NIL is fraught with complex contracts, legal considerations, marketing strategies, and financial implications. Your education can provide the knowledge necessary to navigate these complexities and maximize your NIL in a manner that is both legally compliant and financially sound.

THE IMPORTANCE OF BALANCE

Understanding the role of education in enhancing your NIL underscores the importance of striking a balance. As an athlete, you must juggle the immediate economic gains from your NIL with the long-term benefits of your education. This balance isn't always easy to strike, but it's vital for your long-term success.

Striking a balance means not neglecting your studies in the pursuit of NIL opportunities. It means recognizing that the economic opportunities presented by your NIL are often fleeting, while the benefits of your education are long-lasting. It also means understanding that maximizing your NIL is not just about capitalizing on your athletic performance but also about leveraging your knowledge and communication skills, which are honed through education.

Practical Steps to Balancing NIL and Education
So, how exactly can you balance your NIL with your education? Here are a few practical steps:

1. **Prioritize Time Management**: One of the essential skills you need to balance your NIL and your

education is effective time management. This involves allocating specific time slots to your studies, your sports practice, and your NIL-related activities.

2. **Seek Academic Support**: Most schools offer academic support services to student athletes, such as tutoring, academic advising, and flexible scheduling. Make sure to utilize these resources to keep up with your academic work.

3. **Leverage Off-Seasons**: Off-seasons provide a great opportunity to focus more on your academics and to take on more intensive courses. Conversely, during your sports season, you can opt for a lighter academic load.

4. **Understand NCAA Rules**: The NCAA has specific rules about the amount of time student athletes are allowed to spend on their sports activities. Make sure you understand these rules and ensure your NIL activities do not conflict with them.

5. **Build a Support Network**: A strong support network—including academic advisors, coaches, mentors, and even fellow student athletes—can provide valuable guidance and encouragement as

you navigate the challenging balance between NIL and education.

6. **Stay Organized**: Use tools and techniques to keep your tasks and responsibilities organized. This could be as simple as maintaining a planner or using productivity apps to manage your assignments, NIL commitments, and other activities.

7. **Keep Your Long-Term Goals in Mind**: Remember that your NIL activities should be a part of your larger life and career goals. This perspective will help you make decisions that align with your academic and career objectives, rather than simply pursuing short-term financial gains.

THE FUTURE OF YOUR EDUCATION AND NIL

As you continue your academic journey while maximizing your NIL, it's essential to think about your future. Some student athletes may have the opportunity to go pro in their respective sports, but many will need to rely on the skills and qualifications obtained through their education to build their careers post-college.

The value of your education extends beyond simply enhancing your NIL during your college years. The skills you gain during this time—communication, critical thinking, problem-solving, and teamwork—are all highly transferable and can benefit you in a multitude of career paths. Additionally, the network you build during your college years can open doors for you in the future, in areas directly or indirectly related to your sport.

Furthermore, your education can provide you with a platform to extend the life of your NIL even after your athletic career. Athletes who are knowledgeable and articulate often have opportunities in sports broadcasting, coaching, motivational speaking, and other roles where their NIL continues to hold value.

In the end, the relationship between your NIL and your education is one of symbiosis. Each enhances the other. By maintaining a balance between the two, you can ensure you're not just maximizing your NIL in the present, but also setting the stage for a prosperous future.

STRATEGIES FOR MANAGING ACADEMIC COMMITMENTS ALONGSIDE NIL RESPONSIBILITIES

Successfully managing academic commitments while also fulfilling NIL responsibilities can seem like a Herculean task. It demands strategic planning, excellent time management skills, and a clear understanding of your priorities.

The following strategies can aid you in maintaining this challenging balance and ensuring both your academic and NIL success.

1. **Understanding Your Responsibilities:** The first step in managing your academic commitments alongside your NIL responsibilities is understanding the demands of each. It's crucial to know what your academic obligations are (assignments, exams, projects, etc.) and to have a clear understanding of your NIL responsibilities (contracts, appearances, social media engagements, etc.). Knowledge of your responsibilities is the foundation upon which you can build a workable schedule.

2. **Prioritize and Plan:** With a clear understanding of your responsibilities, the next step is to prioritize. This involves identifying the most important tasks and focusing on those first. It also means planning your time effectively, with

a schedule that allocates specific time slots to academics, athletics, and NIL responsibilities.

3. **Use Available Resources**: Universities often have resources available to help student athletes manage their academic commitments. These can include academic advisors, tutors, study groups, flexible class schedules, and other services. Additionally, consider seeking the help of a manager or agent who understands NIL obligations and can help navigate contracts and scheduling.

4. **Master Time Management**: Time management is a crucial skill for balancing academic and NIL commitments. This involves not only creating a schedule but also sticking to it. Using time management tools and techniques can be immensely helpful in this regard.

5. **Cultivate Self-Discipline**: It's easy to be distracted by the potential immediate rewards of NIL opportunities and neglect academic commitments. Cultivating self-discipline helps you stay focused on long-term goals, enabling you to resist the lure of short-term gratification and keep your attention on your academic obligations.

6. **Communicate Effectively**: Open communication with your professors, coaches, and NIL partners about your multiple commitments can help manage expectations and prevent misunderstandings. This can also foster relationships that are based on mutual respect and understanding.

THE LONG-TERM BENEFITS OF EDUCATION FOR NIL SUCCESS

While it's easy to focus on the immediate economic gains that NIL can bring, it's essential to recognize the long-term benefits that a solid education provides for NIL success. Here are some ways that education can contribute to your NIL value over the long term:

1. **Provides a Solid Foundation**: Education gives you the tools to understand the business, legal, and financial aspects of your NIL. This knowledge can help you navigate the complexities of the NIL world, make informed decisions, and safeguard your interests.

2. **Enhances Communication Skills**: A strong educational background can help you develop excellent communication skills. These skills are vital

when dealing with brands, media, fans, and other stakeholders in your NIL.

3. **Cultivates a Wider Perspective**: Education cultivates a broader worldview and the ability to think critically. This perspective can help you relate to a wider audience, recognize trends, and make smart decisions about your NIL.

4. **Offers Career Opportunities Post-Athletics**: Your athletic career has a finite lifespan, and your education can open doors to opportunities post-athletics where your NIL still holds value. These can include roles in sports broadcasting, coaching, consulting, public speaking, and more.

5. **Builds Personal Brand**: Education contributes to your personal brand, not just as an athlete, but as an intelligent and well-rounded individual. This personal brand can enhance your appeal to different brands and audiences, adding to your NIL value.

6. **Ensures Long-Term Financial Security**: Finally, your education can contribute to long-term financial security. The money from NIL can

be significant, but unpredictable, whereas the financial benefits of a solid education tend to be more reliable and lasting. Your education can lead to stable employment and provide you with the financial skills needed to manage and invest your earnings wisely.

7. **Promotes Resilience**: Education can also offer you a level of resilience in your career. This is particularly true in the case of unexpected life changes, such as an injury that affects your ability to compete. Having a solid educational foundation can give you a safety net, providing other career options if your athletic journey takes an unexpected turn.

8. **Develops Transferable Skills**: Universities are breeding grounds for an array of valuable life skills. Leadership, teamwork, time management, adaptability, problem-solving—these are all competencies you develop as a student, and they can translate into significant advantages in your NIL activities.

Balancing NIL opportunities with your education is not just about maintaining eligibility or graduating. It's about setting yourself up for long-term success. The money that comes from NIL opportunities can be substantial, but it's the education that helps you to maximize those opportunities and ensures that you're well-prepared for the future, regardless of what it may bring.

TIME MANAGEMENT: JUGGLING EDUCATIONAL DEMANDS AND NIL OPPORTUNITIES

Daily Schedule
- 6:00 am – Wake-up
- 6:30 am – Team Breakfast
- 7:00 am – Conditioning Training
- 7:30 am – Shower
- 8:00 am – US History 300
- 9:00 am – Intro to Calculus
- 11:30 am – Team Study Group
- 12:00 pm – Lunch
- 3:00 pm – Practice
- 6:00 pm – Team Dinner/Film Review
- 8:00 pm – Homework
- 10:00 pm – Sleep

Achieving success in both the academic and NIL realms requires a delicate balancing act, at the heart of which lies effective time management. Indeed, without a firm grasp of time management techniques, the demands of these two aspects of your life can seem overwhelming. Here, we will break down some effective strategies that can help you manage your time wisely and successfully juggle your educational and NIL obligations.

1. **Develop a Regular Schedule:** The first step in successful time management is developing a regular schedule. This includes mapping out all of your commitments, from classes and study time to workouts and games, as well as obligations arising from your NIL, such as photoshoots, appearances, social media management, and meetings with your representation.

2. **Prioritize Tasks:** Not every task carries the same weight. Assess the urgency and importance of your tasks and prioritize them accordingly. Tools like the Eisenhower Matrix can help you decide what tasks require immediate attention, which ones you can schedule for later, which ones you can delegate, and which ones you can eliminate.

3. **Make Use of Downtime:** Efficient time management involves making the most of every available moment. Downtime between classes, during travel, or before practice can be used to review class notes, respond to emails related to your NIL, or plan social media content.

4. **Learn to Say No**: While it's important to seize NIL opportunities, remember that you can't do everything. Recognize your limits and learn to say no when necessary. Turning down opportunities that don't align with your brand or could overwhelm your schedule is a key aspect of successful time management.

5. **Leverage Technology**: There are numerous tools and apps available that can help you manage your time effectively. From calendar apps to project management tools, and even social media scheduling platforms, technology can help you stay organized and streamline your tasks.

6. **Seek Support**: Remember that you're not alone. Make use of the support systems available to you, such as academic advisors, coaches, and even personal managers, to help manage your time effectively. They can provide guidance, help you stay accountable, and even assist in coordinating your various commitments.

7. **Stay Flexible**: While a regular schedule is important, it's equally crucial to remain flexible. Unforeseen circumstances can arise, and the ability to adapt

your schedule when needed is an essential part of effective time management.

CASE STUDIES: ATHLETES SUCCESSFULLY BALANCING EDUCATION AND NIL

To provide some inspiration and practical examples, let's explore case studies of athletes who have successfully balanced their education with their NIL opportunities.

Case Study 1: Spencer Lee (Wrestling)

A standout wrestler at the University of Iowa, Spencer Lee managed to excel in both his academic pursuits and his NIL opportunities. Lee won the NCAA Wrestling Championship a number of times while also earning a degree in Sports and Recreation Management. He also became one of the first college athletes to launch his own brand following the changes to the NIL rules, selling merchandise and partnering with brands that align with his values. Lee managed to juggle these responsibilities by maintaining a rigorous schedule and taking advantage of the support systems at his university.

Case Study 2: Paige Bueckers (Basketball)

Paige Bueckers, a star basketball player at the University of Connecticut, has made headlines both for her prowess on the court and her successful navigation of NIL opportunities. Despite her busy athletic schedule, Bueckers has maintained high academic standards. In addition to this, she has landed lucrative endorsement deals and even launched her own basketball camp for young girls. Bueckers attributes her success in balancing these responsibilities to her commitment to time management and her use of technology to stay organized.

Case Study 3: D'Eriq King (Football)

D'Eriq King, the quarterback for the University of Miami, is another excellent example of an athlete balancing education and NIL opportunities. Majoring in Sociology, King has managed to maintain his academic commitments while also becoming one of the first collegiate athletes to sign an endorsement deal following the NIL changes. By utilizing a management team to handle his NIL obligations and maintaining a clear focus on his education, King has set a standard for future athletes navigating the new NIL landscape.

Case Study 4: Haley and Hanna Cavinder (Basketball)

Twin sisters Haley and Hanna Cavinder, basketball players at the University of Miami, have managed to turn their social media popularity into a lucrative part of their NIL strategy without compromising their education. They major in Business and use their knowledge to boost their brand's effectiveness. Their strategy has landed them partnerships with companies like Boost Mobile and Six Star Pro Nutrition. By pre-planning and scheduling their social media content, they have managed to maintain their academic performance while fully embracing their NIL opportunities.

Case Study 5: Olivia Dunne (Gymnastics)

Olivia Dunne, an LSU gymnast, has garnered significant attention on social media, boasting over a million followers on Instagram alone. Despite her online fame and NIL-related commitments, she's still a full-time student at Louisiana State University. Dunne leverages her platform to collaborate with brands that resonate with her followers, such as activewear and fitness products, without compromising her studies. She attributes her ability to maintain a balance to careful planning, leveraging her social media expertise, and assistance from a social media management team.

Case Study 6: Ziyah Holman (Track and Field)

Ziyah Holman, a track and field sprinter at the University of Michigan, is another great example of an athlete successfully managing academic responsibilities alongside NIL opportunities. Despite her continuing studies, she signed a groundbreaking NIL deal with Naomi Osaka's KINLÒ, while also partnering with a meal prep company, all while maintaining high academic standards. Her success lies in her strategic choice of partnerships that not only align with her brand but also support her athletic performance, while keeping a strict schedule to ensure her academics do not suffer.

Case Study 7: Sedona Prince (Basketball)
A University of Oregon basketball player, Sedona Prince gained national attention when her social media post about the disparity between men's and women's facilities at the NCAA tournament went viral. Majoring in Human Dimensions of Organizations, she has been able to leverage her newfound fame into NIL deals with companies like the beverage company Riff, while continuing her education. Prince credits her success to her support network, her strategic approach to NIL opportunities, and her commitment to using her platform for advocacy.

Each of these athletes provides a unique example of how education and NIL opportunities can be successfully balanced. While each journey is unique, some common threads can be observed: maintaining a rigorous and well-planned schedule, utilizing support systems, embracing technology, and staying flexible and adaptable. By implementing these strategies, you too can unlock the power of your NIL while achieving academic success.

Remember, even from these examples, it's clear that there is no single path to success; instead, each athlete must carve out their own unique journey based on their circumstances, values, and goals. These stories can provide a road map as you navigate your own NIL journey, but remember that your path will be uniquely yours. You have the power to shape it in the way that best suits your individual needs and aspirations.

SEVEN

DO YOU NEED A FINANCIAL BACKER?

A s an athlete navigating the new frontier of Name, Image, and Likeness rights, one of the many questions you might ask yourself is, *Do I need a financial backer?* As with any business endeavor, having a financial backer or investor can offer benefits, such as access to capital, valuable contacts, and business expertise. This chapter will delve into the role and importance of financial backers in NIL, their potential benefits and drawbacks, and the considerations that should guide your decision in seeking financial backing.

THE ROLE AND IMPORTANCE OF FINANCIAL BACKERS IN NIL

To understand the role of financial backers in NIL, let's first understand who they are. A financial backer could be an individual or an organization that provides financial support to an athlete to help them further their brand and expand their earning potential. This support could come in the form of direct financial investment, sponsorship deals, endorsement contracts, or other types of financial arrangements.

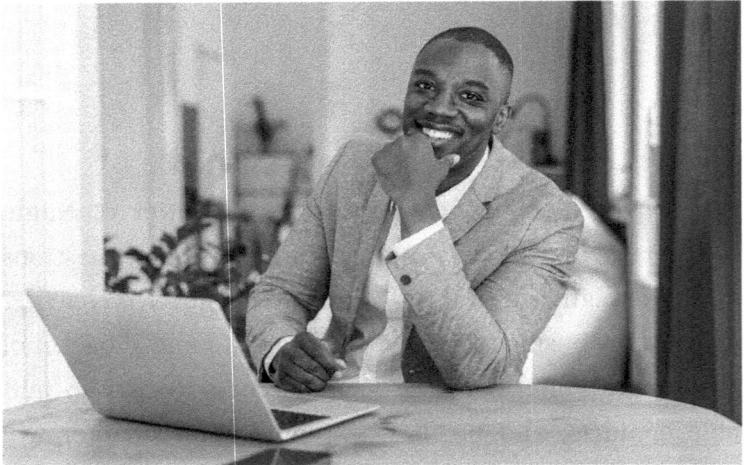

One significant role that financial backers can play in NIL is providing athletes with the funds they need to develop and promote their brand. This might involve costs related to marketing, branding, legal advice, or other expenses associated with maximizing your NIL value. For instance, a financial backer might fund a professional photo shoot for your social media platforms, pay for an expert to design your logo or website, or cover the cost of legal advice regarding NIL contracts.

Another critical role of financial backers is offering athletes access to a broader network. A financial backer with ties to the business or sports industry might be able to connect you with valuable contacts, such as potential sponsors, brand partners, or other business opportunities. These relationships could be vital in broadening your NIL opportunities and increasing your earning potential.

Finally, financial backers might also bring business expertise that can be invaluable for athletes. Understanding how to negotiate contracts, identify promising opportunities, manage risk, and navigate the financial aspects of NIL can be challenging, especially for young athletes who are new to the business world. A financial backer with business experience can offer advice, guidance, and mentorship to help athletes make informed decisions about their NIL strategy.

POTENTIAL BENEFITS AND DRAWBACKS OF FINANCIAL BACKERS

There are several potential benefits of having a financial backer:

1. **Access to Capital**: This is the most apparent advantage. With financial backing, you have more

resources at your disposal to invest in your brand, whether that's through marketing, hiring experts, or other brand-enhancing strategies.

2. **Access to Expertise**: A financial backer with business or sports industry experience can provide invaluable advice and mentorship.

3. **Networking Opportunities**: Financial backers often have extensive networks and can provide introductions to potential sponsors, brand partners, or other valuable contacts.

4. **Risk Mitigation**: Having a financial backer can reduce the financial risk associated with investing in your brand. If your efforts are unsuccessful, you're not shouldering the financial loss alone.

However, there can also be drawbacks:

1. **Loss of Control**: Depending on your agreement, a financial backer may want a say in your NIL decisions, potentially limiting your control over your own brand.

2. **Profit Sharing**: Any profits from your NIL activities might have to be shared with your backer.

3. **Increased Pressure**: With someone else's money at stake, you might feel additional pressure to succeed, which could lead to stress or hasty decision-making.

MAKING THE DECISION: DO YOU NEED A FINANCIAL BACKER?

The decision to seek a financial backer is highly personal and should be based on careful consideration of your individual circumstances, goals, and values. Here are some key factors to consider:

1. **Your Financial Needs**: Do you have the resources you need to invest in your brand? Developing a brand takes not only time and effort but also money. You may need to hire a team of professionals, from photographers and website designers to marketing specialists and lawyers. If your current financial situation doesn't allow for this level of investment, you may benefit from having a financial backer.

2. **Your Access to Networks and Expertise**: If you already have strong networks within the sports and business industries and feel confident in your understanding of NIL rights and the business world, you may not need the additional connections and

guidance a financial backer can provide. On the other hand, if you feel isolated or overwhelmed, having a financial backer with the right connections and expertise could be extremely beneficial.

3. **Your Tolerance for Risk**: Seeking financial backing can reduce the personal financial risk associated with investing in your brand. However, it also introduces new risks, such as the potential loss of control over your brand or the pressure of having someone else's money at stake. You'll need to weigh these risks against the potential benefits.

4. **Your Long-term Goals**: Are you planning to capitalize on your NIL rights as much as possible while you're in college, or do you see this as a long-term endeavor that will continue throughout your professional career and beyond? If your goals are more short-term, you may not need a financial backer. If you're looking at the long game, a financial backer could provide the support you need to build and sustain a successful brand over time.

Remember, every athlete's situation is different, and what works for one person might not work for another. It's essential to seek advice from trusted mentors, family members, and professionals before making any significant decisions about your NIL strategy.

SELECTING THE RIGHT FINANCIAL BACKER: KEY CONSIDERATIONS

Choosing a financial backer is a significant decision that can have far-reaching implications for your NIL exploitation journey. Here are some key considerations to keep in mind:

1. **Shared Vision:** It's essential to find a backer who understands and supports your vision for your brand. This shared understanding can reduce conflicts and ensure a smoother working relationship.

2. **Relevant Experience:** Look for backers with experience in the sports industry and a track record of success in brand building and NIL exploitation. This experience can be invaluable as you navigate the business side of your athletic career.

3. **Networking Potential:** Consider the backer's network within the sports and business industries. Can they connect you with opportunities and resources that would otherwise be inaccessible?

4. **Agreeable Terms**: Be sure to scrutinize any proposed financial agreement to ensure the terms are agreeable. Pay close attention to aspects like profit-sharing ratios, decision-making authority, and exit clauses.

5. **Personal Chemistry**: You'll likely be working closely with your backer, so it's important to have good personal chemistry. This mutual respect and understanding can make for a more enjoyable and successful working relationship.

Remember, engaging a financial backer is not a decision to be taken lightly. Weigh the pros and cons carefully and take the time to select a backer who aligns with your vision, brings valuable expertise to the table, and has terms and conditions you can comfortably agree with. This careful consideration will help ensure a more successful and rewarding NIL exploitation journey.

BUILDING AND MANAGING A RELATIONSHIP WITH YOUR FINANCIAL BACKER

When you have decided to bring on a financial backer, building a strong relationship becomes an imperative part of the equation. Navigating this relationship requires a thoughtful approach, and the initial stages of interaction are crucial.

1. **Establishing Open Communication**: The foundation of any good relationship, including that with your financial backer, lies in open, honest communication. Be transparent about your goals, expectations, and concerns right from the beginning. Frequent and structured communication is also necessary to keep your backer updated about your activities and progress. Regular updates make the backer feel involved and appreciated and can pave the way for constructive feedback.

2. **Developing Mutual Trust**: Building trust with your financial backer takes time and effort. Consistently delivering on your commitments, maintaining transparency, and demonstrating your passion for and dedication to your sport are excellent ways to build trust.

3. **Working Toward Shared Goals**: It's essential that you and your backer align on the strategic vision and goals for your brand. Regular discussions on your NIL strategy can help ensure that you're both working toward the same objectives.

4. **Resolving Conflicts Constructively**: Disagreements are inevitable in any relationship.

What's important is how you handle these conflicts. Always approach disagreements with respect and a willingness to understand the other person's perspective. Finding a mutually acceptable solution should always be the aim.

5. **Fostering Personal Connections**: While your relationship with your financial backer is primarily professional, cultivating a personal connection can foster stronger bonds. Understanding and appreciating your backer's motivations and interests can lead to a more harmonious and successful relationship.

RESOURCE MANAGEMENT: UTILIZING BACKERS FOR NIL SUCCESS

As we just showed you, financial backers are more than just a source of capital; they can be valuable resources that can greatly contribute to your NIL success. Here's how to utilize them effectively:

1. **Leverage Their Business Acumen**: A financial backer with business experience can provide priceless advice and guidance. From strategic decision-making to negotiating contracts, their

expertise can help you navigate the business side of NIL exploitation more effectively.

2. **Benefit from Their Network**: Your backer's professional network can offer a wealth of opportunities. Whether it's introductions to key industry players, access to marketing resources, or potential collaborations, these connections can greatly enhance your NIL journey.

3. **Utilize Their Financial Expertise**: Your backer's financial knowledge can be instrumental in managing and growing your NIL earnings. They can offer guidance on budgeting, financial planning, and investing, helping you secure a more financially stable future.

4. **Collaborate on Marketing and Promotion**: A backer who understands marketing can collaborate with you on promotional strategies for your brand. Their insights can help you create effective marketing campaigns, enhance your public image, and ultimately, maximize your NIL value.

CASE STUDIES: ATHLETES WITH
SUCCESSFUL FINANCIAL BACKING

Let's explore the journeys of several athletes who have harnessed the power of financial backing to maximize their NIL opportunities.

Case Study 1:
Michael Jordan

The story of Michael Jordan and Nike is the epitome of a successful athlete-financial backer relationship. Jordan partnered with Nike in 1984, a move that would revolutionize athlete endorsements and the sneaker industry. The resulting Air Jordan brand has earned Jordan over $1.3 billion since its inception, demonstrating the monumental impact a strategic partnership with a financial backer can have on an athlete's NIL value.

Case Study 2: LeBron James

LeBron James, one of the biggest names in the NBA, has turned his NIL into a vast empire with the help of strategic financial backing. His relationship with Nike, which started with a $90 million contract in his rookie year, continued to evolve, leading to a lifetime deal reportedly worth over

$1 billion. James has also attracted financial backing from companies like Coca-Cola and Upper Deck, significantly boosting his NIL value.

Case Study 3: Serena Williams

As one of the most successful tennis players of all time, Serena Williams has attracted significant financial backing throughout her career. Her endorsement portfolio includes partnerships with Nike, Gatorade, and Beats by Dre. Furthermore, she has leveraged financial backing to establish her own clothing line, Serena, showcasing the potential for athletes to create personal brands with the right financial support.

Case Study 4: Peyton Manning

NFL legend Peyton Manning provides an excellent example of maximizing NIL value through financial backing. Manning's endorsements span a variety of industries, from Nationwide Insurance to Papa John's Pizza, earning him an estimated $150 million over his career. Manning's strategy involved partnerships that allowed him to showcase his brand, humor, and relatability, proving that aligning NIL exploitation with personal strengths can lead to monumental success.

Case Study 5: Simone Biles

Olympic gymnast Simone Biles has leveraged financial backing to boost her NIL value. Her partnerships include brands such as Nike, Kellogg's, and Hershey's. Biles' partnerships not only support her financially but also amplify her role as a role model for young athletes, demonstrating how athletes can use NIL opportunities to enhance their brand.

Case Study 6: Cristiano Ronaldo

Soccer star Cristiano Ronaldo, one of the highest-earning athletes in the world, has utilized financial backing to maximize his NIL value. His partnerships include lucrative deals with Nike, Herbalife, and KFC. Ronaldo's large social media following provides immense value to his backers, highlighting the importance of digital presence in enhancing NIL opportunities.

Case Study 7: Alex Morgan

Women's soccer player Alex Morgan is another example of an athlete successfully harnessing financial backing. Morgan has partnerships with companies like Nike, Coca-Cola, and McDonald's. These partnerships not only offer financial support but also contribute to her mission of advancing the visibility of women's sports.

Each of these athletes has utilized financial backing in their own unique way, demonstrating the versatility and potential of NIL exploitation. As we see in these examples, the relationship between an athlete and a financial backer can be incredibly mutually beneficial, leading to financial success for the athlete and positive brand association for the backer. Whether through clothing lines, endorsements, or digital presence, each of these athletes has leveraged financial backing to create a personal brand and maximize their NIL value.

STAYING INFORMED AND CONNECTED

As we wrap up this chapter, it's crucial to remember that the world of Name, Image, and Likeness is a dynamic and rapidly evolving landscape. To help you stay updated and connected, we've innovatively included an index of agents and managers who specialize in NIL. Instead of presenting this as a static list that might quickly become outdated, we have provided this index as a QR code. By scanning the QR code, you can access the most current information about these professionals in real time. This resource will help you effectively navigate your NIL journey, ensuring you have access to the best expertise and support when you need it. This is one more tool in your toolkit as you explore the new frontier of NIL rights and opportunities.

EIGHT

INJURIES AND NIL

njuries are an unfortunate reality in the world of sports, often striking unpredictably and carrying potential implications for an athlete's NIL value. It is therefore essential for athletes to understand how they can mitigate the impact of injuries on their NIL.

Injuries can, in certain cases, result in reduced playing time, negatively affecting an athlete's visibility and performance, two factors that significantly contribute to NIL value. For instance, a star player who sustains a severe injury might be sidelined for an extended period, consequently impacting their public visibility and performance statistics. This could lead to reduced interest from brands or sponsors, thereby affecting the athlete's NIL-related income.

However, it's crucial to remember that athletes are not valued solely for their on-field performances. Their appeal often stems from their personal stories, struggles, and triumphs. An athlete's comeback journey after an injury can be compelling, appealing to fans' emotions and potentially attracting brands that value resilience, perseverance, and determination. Thus, the way an athlete manages their injury and communicates it to their fans can greatly influence their NIL value.

Moreover, an athlete's off-field activities can significantly contribute to their NIL value. Athletes can participate in community service, personal branding efforts, or pursue personal passions, all of which can maintain or even enhance their NIL value during injury spells. Off-field contributions can also strengthen an athlete's relationship with their fans, sponsors, and the community, which can serve to bolster NIL's value.

Ultimately, the goal should be to establish a personal brand that transcends on-field performance, providing value to fans and sponsors irrespective of injuries or performance fluctuations. This involves consistent and authentic engagement with fans, proactive and strategic personal branding, and maintaining a strong digital presence.

MANAGING NIL CONTRACTS AMID INJURIES

Handling NIL contracts amid injuries can be a complex and challenging process, requiring a strong understanding of contractual obligations and the potential implications of an injury. An injury might affect an athlete's ability to fulfill certain obligations, such as appearances, performances, or product promotions, which can have legal and financial consequences.

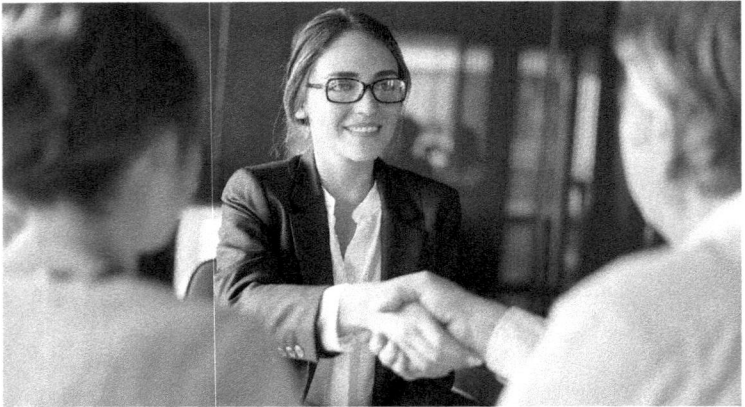

It's important to consider potential injuries while negotiating NIL contracts, including clauses that provide protection in case of an injury. Such clauses might involve insurance coverages, obligations in case of injury, or the ability to renegotiate terms in light of significant injuries. Professional legal advice can be invaluable in navigating these aspects.

Furthermore, open communication with sponsors or brands is crucial in the event of an injury. This allows for collaborative problem-solving and the opportunity to modify contractual obligations in a manner that suits both parties. In some cases, the athlete might be able to offer alternative forms of value, such as social media promotions or personal appearances, which can help maintain the NIL relationship despite the injury.

It's also essential for athletes to understand their insurance coverage, including what is covered, the process for filing claims, and the potential impact on their NIL income. Professional advice can be beneficial in understanding these elements and ensuring the athlete is adequately protected.

Additionally, whenever there is hardship, there is also opportunity. Consider this the key moment to represent a large physical therapy company, a renowned surgeon, the latest rehabilitation equipment, or any other industry that you encounter along your journey of repairing your body and healing from an injury. No matter the situation, there is always a place for a positive influence through a sound business relationship.

RISK MANAGEMENT STRATEGIES FOR STUDENT ATHLETES

In any industry, understanding and managing risks are essential components of success. For athletes, these risks can range from injuries, poor performance, and scandals, to contractual disputes, all of which can impact their NIL value. Therefore, adopting comprehensive risk management strategies is paramount.

One of the key risk management strategies for athletes involves maintaining a positive public image. Athletes' behaviors both on and off the field can significantly impact their NIL value. Thus, they should uphold high standards of professionalism, adopt positive lifestyle choices, and avoid controversial actions or statements that could harm their reputation.

Another critical strategy is ensuring that their NIL contracts are fair and transparent. Athletes should engage the services of legal experts when negotiating contracts to understand the potential risks and safeguard their interests. This includes understanding the terms and conditions, potential liabilities, and the parties' obligations. In the event of a dispute, legal counsel can provide valuable guidance, reducing the potential negative impact on the athlete's NIL value.

Diversification is a valuable risk management strategy. Athletes should not rely on a single source for their NIL value but instead diversify their engagements, income sources, and partnerships. This could include various endorsements, personal businesses, media appearances, and investments. Such diversification can insulate athletes from fluctuations in NIL value, ensuring a stable income stream.

Finally, athletes should invest in their physical and mental health as part of their risk management strategy. Regular check-ups, proper nutrition, adequate rest, and psychological support can help prevent injuries, enhance performance, and boost mental resilience. As physical performance and mental well-being can significantly affect an athlete's NIL value, prioritizing health is an effective risk management strategy.

INSURANCE CONSIDERATIONS FOR PROTECTING NIL

Insurance plays a crucial role in protecting an athlete's NIL value. Given the inherent risks associated with sports, including the potential for career-ending injuries, athletes must understand the different types of insurance available and the coverage they provide.

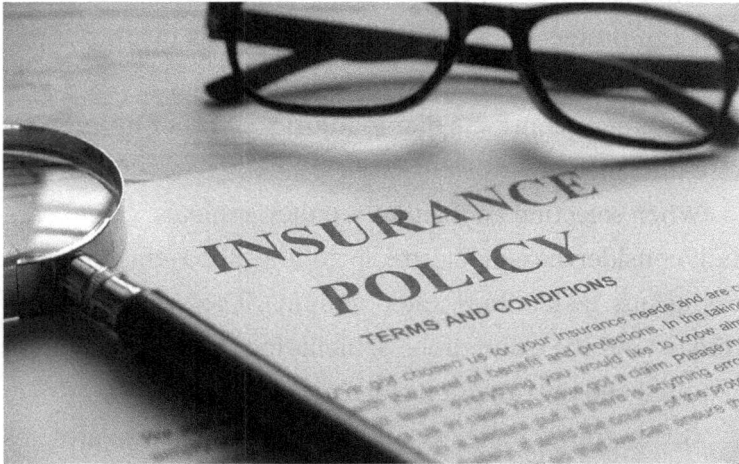

Disability insurance is one of the essential coverages for athletes. This type of insurance provides financial protection if an athlete suffers an injury or illness that prevents them from competing. The policy usually covers a portion of the athlete's projected future income, which can include potential NIL earnings.

Another type of insurance that athletes may consider is loss of value (LOV) insurance. LOV insurance is designed to protect athletes who may suffer a significant drop in their draft position due to an injury or illness. This coverage can supplement disability insurance by covering the difference between the athlete's expected professional contract and the lower amount they may receive due to their drop in the draft.

Endorsement insurance is another type of coverage that can protect an athlete's NIL value. This insurance protects against losses resulting from the inability to fulfill endorsement contracts due to injuries or other unforeseen circumstances.

When selecting an insurance policy, athletes should carefully consider the policy terms, including the coverage amount, exclusions, deductibles, and premiums. It's also important to understand the claim process, including the documentation required and the timeframe for claim settlement.

Given the complexity of insurance matters, athletes should consider engaging a professional insurance advisor or attorney. These professionals can provide valuable advice, helping athletes understand their insurance needs and navigate the selection process. This investment can provide invaluable protection for an athlete's NIL value, safeguarding their financial future in the face of unexpected events.

HEALTH MANAGEMENT: NAVIGATING INJURIES FOR NIL LONGEVITY

Physical injuries are a part of every athlete's life, but how you manage them can determine the trajectory of your career, including your NIL value. Effective health management and careful navigation of injuries can allow athletes to extend their career longevity, maintain their performance levels, and thereby preserve or even enhance their NIL value.

First and foremost, a proactive approach to injury prevention is paramount. This involves adhering to a consistent routine of physical conditioning, including strength training, cardiovascular exercise, and flexibility work. The integration of rest days and adequate sleep into this routine is also crucial, as these factors contribute significantly to recovery and the prevention of overuse injuries. Additionally, a balanced, nutrient-rich diet can optimize energy levels and facilitate quicker recovery from injuries.

In the event of an injury, prompt and appropriate treatment is critical. This includes immediate medical attention and adherence to prescribed rehabilitation programs. While the desire to return to competition can be strong, rushing the healing process can lead to further damage and long-term complications, negatively impacting an athlete's performance and NIL value. Therefore, athletes should prioritize full recovery and consult with healthcare professionals before returning to their sport.

Mental health also plays a significant role in navigating injuries. The psychological impact of injury, including stress, frustration, and fear of reinjury, can be profound and may affect an athlete's performance and recovery. Athletes should consider engaging with sports psychologists or counselors to help manage these aspects of injury and recovery.

Finally, communicating effectively with fans and the public during injury periods can help maintain an athlete's NIL value. Transparent communication about the injury, treatment progress, and expected return can keep fans engaged and supportive. Furthermore, sharing the journey of overcoming adversity can enhance an athlete's image and deepen the connection with their audience.

CASE STUDIES: OVERCOMING INJURIES
WHILE MAINTAINING NIL VALUE

Case Study 1: Paul George

In 2014, NBA player Paul George suffered a devastating leg injury during a scrimmage for the US national team. Despite the gruesome injury, George was able to maintain his NIL value. His perseverance and determination during his recovery journey resonated with fans, enhancing his image as a resilient and dedicated athlete. Furthermore, he was able to return to an All-Star level of play, further solidifying his NIL value.

Case Study 2: Serena Williams

The tennis icon has overcome numerous injuries throughout her career, demonstrating an unrivaled resilience that has not only sustained but also amplified her NIL value. Her strength, both on and off the court, has made her an inspiration to many and a powerful influencer.

Case Study 3: Alex Smith

The NFL quarterback suffered a life-threatening leg injury in 2018, but his extraordinary comeback story captivated fans worldwide and preserved his NIL value. The ESPN documentary "Project 11," which chronicled Smith's injury and recovery, further showcased his journey, building an emotional connection with fans.

Case Study 4: Bethany Hamilton

The professional surfer lost her left arm in a shark attack but returned to professional surfing just one year later. Her inspiring story was chronicled in the film Soul Surfer, elevating her NIL value and turning her into a global icon of resilience and determination.

Case Study 5: Peyton Manning

After undergoing multiple neck surgeries, many questioned whether Manning could return to his MVP form. Not only did he return to the NFL, but he also led the Denver Broncos to a Super Bowl victory. Manning's successful comeback, coupled with his strong personal brand, ensured his NIL value remained high.

Case Study 6: Lindsey Vonn

The World Cup alpine ski racer has sustained multiple severe injuries throughout her career. Despite this, her NIL value remained strong, primarily due to her success on the slopes, charismatic personality, and openness about her struggles and recovery. Her resilience inspired many and cemented her status as one of the greatest female skiers of all time.

Case Study 7: Conor McGregor

The outspoken MMA fighter has had his share of physical trials, including a significant leg break in 2021. However, his confident persona, consistent interaction with his fans, and active participation in various business ventures have allowed him to maintain a strong NIL value. His successful whiskey brand, Proper No. Twelve is a testament to how an athlete can leverage their NIL beyond their sports career.

These case studies illustrate the importance of proper injury management, mental fortitude, and effective communication in maintaining NIL value during injury periods. They also highlight the potential of an injury experience to deepen the connection with fans, inspire many, and solidify an athlete's image and brand.

As you can see, injuries don't necessarily have to diminish an athlete's NIL value. While they pose a significant challenge, careful navigation and management of these injuries, coupled with resilience and effective communication, can help athletes maintain or even enhance their NIL value during these periods. The key lies in seeing the injury not as a debilitating event but as an opportunity to showcase resilience, determination, and humanity that fans and the public can relate to.

By recognizing the potential of unexpected events like injuries to disrupt their careers, athletes can adopt strategies that allow them to mitigate these risks and safeguard their NIL value. Incorporating diverse elements into their personal brand, planning for financial security, and staying informed about relevant legal developments are all part of this strategy. By doing so, they can ensure their NIL continues to thrive, regardless of what the future holds.

— NINE —

NIL VALUATIONS AND FINANCIAL MANAGEMENT

The NIL of an athlete constitute a significant portion of their market value, particularly in the era of social media and widespread connectivity. But how is this value determined? How can an athlete or their team translate popularity and reputation into a financial figure? This chapter provides a comprehensive overview of the factors and methodologies that contribute to the valuation of NIL, guiding athletes to a more nuanced understanding of their worth and providing actionable insights for effective financial management.

FACTORS AFFECTING NIL VALUATION

NIL valuations hinge on numerous elements, some quantifiable, others less tangible. Together, they create a holistic impression of an athlete's market value.

Some of these factors include:

1. **Performance**: An athlete's on-field performance significantly impacts their NIL value. Achievements, consistency, and potential for growth are all scrutinized by potential sponsors.

2. **Media Presence**: Athletes who frequently appear in media have higher visibility, which can translate to increased NIL value. This includes traditional media

like TV and newspapers, as well as digital media platforms like YouTube and podcasts.

3. **Social Media Engagement**: A strong social media presence is invaluable in the modern era. It's not just about the number of followers but also engagement level—likes, shares, comments, and the overall interaction with posts. High engagement signifies an active and dedicated fan base, which is attractive to sponsors.

4. **Personal Brand**: This encapsulates the athlete's image, values, and lifestyle. A personal brand can be significantly bolstered by community involvement, philanthropic activities, and having a unique, authentic persona that resonates with fans.

5. **Market Size**: An athlete's geographic location or the popularity of their sport can influence their market size. Athletes in larger markets or popular sports often have higher NIL values.

6. **Demographics**: Age, gender, and ethnicity can affect NIL values as they can appeal to different target markets for potential sponsors.

METHODOLOGIES FOR VALUING NIL

Given the complexity of these factors, several methodologies are used to quantify NIL value, usually involving a combination of market research, statistical analysis, and financial modeling. Here are a few commonly used approaches:

1. **Comparable Transactions**: This approach involves analyzing recent deals involving athletes with similar characteristics. Factors such as sport, performance level, market size, and demographics are considered.

2. **Market Research**: Surveys and focus groups can gauge public perception of an athlete and their potential appeal to different target markets. This can provide valuable insights for valuation.

3. **Social Media Analytics**: Digital tools can analyze an athlete's social media presence, track engagement, and estimate potential reach, providing concrete data for valuation.

4. **Income Approach**: This methodology forecasts the potential income an athlete could generate from their NIL, including sponsorship deals, merchandise

sales, and appearance fees. These forecasts are then discounted back to their present value.

THE ROLE OF AGENTS AND MANAGERS IN NIL VALUATIONS

The valuation of an athlete's NIL is a complex process, one which often calls for expert guidance. This is where agents and managers come into play. They have the expertise and industry knowledge to help athletes navigate the intricate landscape of NIL valuations.

UNDERSTANDING THE BASICS: AGENTS VS. MANAGERS

While people often use the terms "agent" and "manager" interchangeably, these roles have different focuses and responsibilities.

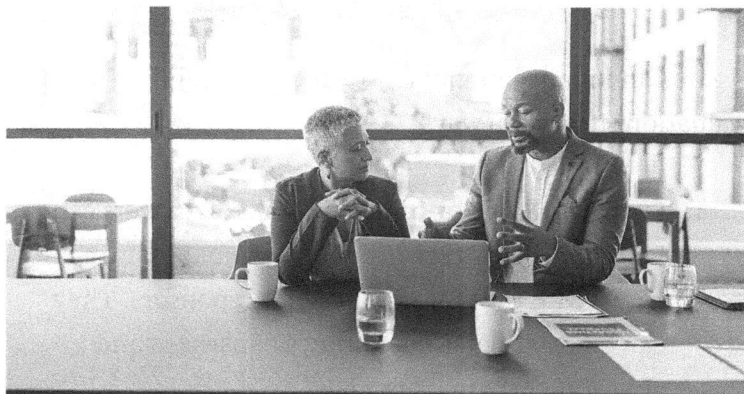

Agents are primarily deal-makers. Their primary task is to find and negotiate contracts for their clients. They liaise between the athlete and potential sponsors, ensuring the athlete receives fair compensation for their NIL rights. Agents must be skilled negotiators, have an in-depth understanding of contract law, and be up-to-date on the going rates for NIL rights in their client's specific sport and market.

Managers, on the other hand, take on a broader role. In addition to overseeing deals, they help shape the athlete's overall career trajectory. This includes managing public relations, steering the athlete's public image, coordinating with the athlete's training schedule, and providing general career guidance. Managers play a significant role in strategically positioning the athlete's NIL for maximum value.

HOW AGENTS AND MANAGERS ENHANCE NIL VALUATIONS

Agents and managers can help athletes maximize their NIL valuations in several ways:

1. **Strategic Positioning**: Agents and managers can help shape an athlete's public persona, ensuring it aligns with the values of potential sponsors. They can guide athletes in crafting a consistent and appealing personal brand.

2. **Access to Opportunities:** Agents have extensive networks within the sports industry, enabling them to identify sponsorship opportunities that athletes might otherwise miss.

3. **Negotiation:** Agents are expert negotiators. Good agents know the ins and outs of contracts and can ensure athletes receive the best possible terms.

4. **Risk Management:** Managers help athletes maintain a positive public image, avoiding scandals or negative press that could harm their NIL value. They also ensure that athletes comply with all relevant NIL regulations, protecting them from potential legal issues.

5. **Career Guidance:** Managers provide long-term career planning, which can enhance an athlete's earning potential over time. They ensure athletes make decisions that align with their long-term financial and personal goals.

CASE STUDIES: NIL VALUATION SUCCESSES AND FAILURES

Understanding the theoretical aspects of NIL valuations is crucial. However, real-life examples provide invaluable lessons, presenting tangible illustrations of how these theories play out in the world of sports. In this section, we examine several case studies, exploring both successful and less successful attempts to maximize NIL valuations.

Success Story: Serena Williams

One of the greatest athletes of all time, Serena Williams has successfully leveraged her NIL to become one of the highest-earning female athletes. Serena's success goes beyond her incredible tennis skills. Her agents and managers have done an outstanding job building her personal brand. Serena's image—a blend of strength, elegance, resilience, and femininity—resonates with a broad audience. This has attracted a diverse range of sponsors, from sports companies like Nike to luxury brands such as Audemars Piguet. Her active social media presence has further amplified her NIL value, allowing her to connect directly with her fans.

A Cautionary Tale: Ryan Lochte

On the flip side, Ryan Lochte provides a cautionary tale of how poor decisions can negatively impact an athlete's NIL value. The decorated Olympic swimmer saw his NIL value plummet after a scandal during the 2016 Rio Olympics. After initially claiming to have been robbed at gunpoint, it emerged that Lochte had fabricated the story to cover up vandalizing a gas station. The incident led to a public relations disaster. Several sponsors, including Speedo and Ralph Lauren, cut ties with Lochte. This instance underscores the crucial role of image management in maintaining and enhancing an athlete's NIL value. A manager's role in guiding athletes and helping them make good decisions can be critical in avoiding such situations.

Success Story: The Williams Sisters
The Williams sisters, Serena and Venus, while they are both individuals, also work as a team. They have both effectively maximized their NIL value throughout their careers. With their excellent performance on the court and charismatic personas off it, they attracted major sponsors like Nike, Wilson, Gatorade, and more. They also leveraged their fame into successful business ventures. Their agents and managers have been instrumental in these successes, helping to negotiate lucrative contracts and advising on sound business decisions. The Williams sisters exemplify how athletic prowess, strong personal branding, and astute management can combine to maximize NIL value.

A Cautionary Tale: Johnny Manziel
Another contrasting example is Johnny Manziel, a former Heisman Trophy–winning quarterback from Texas A&M. Despite having high NIL value during his college career and a promising start in the NFL, Manziel's personal issues

led to a series of problems, including being dropped by the Cleveland Browns and his sponsor, Nike. Although he had the potential for high NIL earnings, his lack of discipline and poor decisions severely impacted his NIL value. Manziel's case emphasizes the importance of personal conduct in maintaining NIL value and the potential risks that come with fame and fortune.

Success Story: Alex Morgan

Another success story is Alex Morgan, an American soccer player, and Olympic gold medalist. Despite women's soccer traditionally receiving less attention and sponsorship investment than men's, Morgan has built a highly lucrative brand. She has endorsement deals with companies like Nike, Coca-Cola, and McDonald's. Her agent's ability to secure these deals despite the challenges facing women's soccer demonstrates the importance of skillful negotiation and strategic positioning in maximizing NIL value.

A Cautionary Tale: Lance Armstrong

Lance Armstrong, once a beloved American cyclist and seven-time Tour de France winner, represents one of the most notable failures in sports NIL history. Armstrong's success on the bike earned him substantial endorsement deals with companies like Nike and Trek. However, his reputation (and NIL value) plummeted when he was found guilty of doping. Sponsors quickly distanced themselves, and he lost millions in potential earnings. Armstrong's case serves as a stark reminder that honesty and integrity play a crucial role in maintaining and enhancing an athlete's NIL value.

Success Story: Naomi Osaka

Naomi Osaka, a professional tennis player, has managed to successfully leverage her NIL. Osaka became a household name after winning multiple Grand Slam tournaments. Beyond her sports prowess, she has used her platform to speak out on important social issues, enhancing her profile and attractiveness to sponsors. She has landed lucrative endorsement deals with big names such as Nike, Nissan, and Mastercard, and at some point, she earned so much in off-court earnings that she was the highest-paid female athlete in the world. Osaka's case shows that a strong personal brand, coupled with sporting excellence can lead to considerable NIL success.

A Cautionary Tale: Adrian Peterson

Adrian Peterson, despite being one of the most talented running backs in the NFL, faced severe financial difficulties due to poor money management. Despite earning over $100 million throughout his career, Peterson found himself in severe debt due to extravagant spending and bad investments. His case highlights the importance of financial literacy and prudent management of earnings derived from NIL.

THE IMPACT OF MARKET TRENDS ON NIL VALUATIONS

The relationship between NIL valuations and market trends is symbiotic. The market in which an athlete operates, both the sporting market and the broader socio-economic market, can dramatically influence the value of an athlete's Name, Image, and Likeness.

Market trends are derived from the ebb and flow of consumer behavior, cultural shifts, technological advances, and economic changes. As a result, they can dramatically shift the appeal of an athlete to potential sponsors and partners, affecting the valuation of their NIL. For instance, athletes involved in sports that suddenly gain popularity can experience a surge in NIL value. Similarly, an athlete's standing can rise if they align themselves with a social cause that's gaining traction or if they utilize emerging platforms that resonate with a desired demographic.

In addition, technological trends can affect NIL valuations. With the advent of social media and online platforms, athletes now have an unprecedented direct line to their fans. Platforms like X (formerly Twitter), Instagram, and Facebook, along with video streaming services like Twitch and YouTube, offer new avenues for athletes to engage with their fans and create personal brands. For example, athletes with strong social media engagement can attract advertisers looking for influencers, increasing their NIL value.

Moreover, market trends related to economic conditions can impact NIL values. During times of economic prosperity, companies might be more willing to invest in athlete endorsements. Conversely, during a recession, these opportunities may dwindle.

However, navigating market trends requires a savvy understanding of these dynamics and an ability to capitalize on opportunities. It's crucial for athletes to stay informed and be adaptable in their strategy to maximize their NIL value.

FINANCIAL MANAGEMENT: UNDERSTANDING YOUR NIL WORTH

Understanding your NIL worth is a critical step in financial management for athletes. It can help in setting realistic expectations, planning for the future, and making informed decisions.

The first step in understanding your NIL worth is getting an accurate valuation. This requires analyzing various factors like your sporting performance, marketability, fan base size, public persona, and engagement rates on social media. Athletes may seek the help of professionals, like sports marketing agencies or consultants, for a more comprehensive assessment.

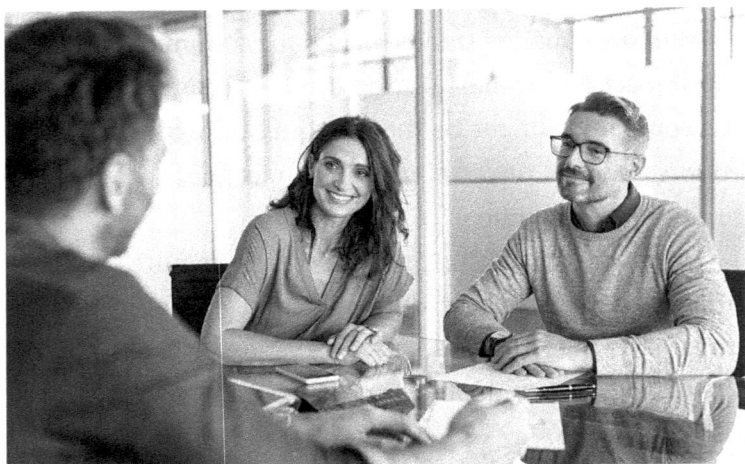

Once you have an estimate of your NIL worth, it's important to manage it properly. This entails a two-pronged approach. On one hand, there's the task of growing your NIL value. This can be achieved by enhancing your sporting performance, building a strong brand, expanding your fan base, and increasing your marketability through various strategies like community involvement, media appearances, or endorsement deals.

On the other hand, there's the task of managing the income generated from your NIL. Athletes need to develop good financial habits and engage in prudent money management. This includes budgeting, saving, investing, and paying taxes. It's advisable to work with financial advisors who specialize in working with athletes. They can provide personalized advice, help avoid common financial pitfalls, and plan for a financially secure future.

Moreover, understanding your NIL worth is a continuous process. With changes in your career and the external market, your NIL value can fluctuate. Regular reassessment and adjustments to your financial plans are therefore necessary. This ongoing process, though it may seem daunting, is crucial to maximizing and preserving your NIL value over time.

Understanding the financial implications of NIL and managing it effectively is critical to not only enhance an athlete's current earnings but also secure their future financial stability. Through a comprehensive understanding of market trends, a keen awareness of personal NIL worth, and effective financial management strategies, athletes can fully unlock the power of their Name, Image, and Likeness.

FUTURE TRENDS AND PREDICTIONS IN NIL VALUATIONS

As the era of Name, Image, and Likeness rights matures, there will likely be several key trends and developments that will influence how NIL valuations are determined in the future. Here are a few predictions and considerations.

1. **Increased Professionalization of NIL Management**: As NIL becomes an increasingly lucrative opportunity, the management of these rights will become more professionalized. Expect to see more agencies and managers specializing in NIL management, providing athletes with expertise and resources to enhance their NIL value. This professionalization will also lead to a more systematic approach to NIL valuations, with standardized models and methodologies being developed.

2. **Technology's Influence on Valuations**: With the growing importance of social media platforms in shaping an athlete's brand, technology will play a significant role in NIL valuations. Metrics such as social media followers, engagement rates, and content virality will factor heavily into valuations. Moreover, advancements in AI and data analytics may allow for more precise and dynamic valuations, taking into account real-time changes in an athlete's popularity and market influence.

3. **Diversification of Revenue Streams**: Future NIL valuations will also likely consider an expanded range of income sources. Besides traditional

endorsements and sponsorships, athletes will generate revenue from personalized merchandise, digital content, virtual fan experiences, e-sports, and more. New technologies, such as blockchain and non-fungible tokens (NFTs), could open up innovative revenue streams, like tokenizing athletes' moments or digital autographs.

4. **Legislative Changes**: The legislative landscape around NIL is still evolving, with states and the federal government ironing out legislation. Changes in these laws could dramatically impact NIL valuations, either by broadening opportunities for athletes or by imposing new restrictions and regulations.

5. **Greater Emphasis on Personal Brand**: As the competition for attention and endorsement deals grows, the differentiation of personal brand will become crucial. Athletes who can establish a unique, authentic, and compelling personal brand will have an advantage, leading to higher NIL valuations. This might include their stance on social issues, personal stories, or unique skills beyond their sporting prowess.

6. **Impact of Globalization**: As the world continues to become more connected, athletes will increasingly have the opportunity to attract fans and sponsors from across the globe. This globalization will open up new markets, and athletes who can appeal to these diverse audiences will see a boost in their NIL value.

7. **Consideration of Long-Term Value**: Future valuations will likely consider an athlete's potential for long-term value creation. This means looking beyond their active sporting career to their potential for ongoing revenue generation through coaching, commentating, product endorsements, or other roles within their sport or beyond.

Predicting future trends is always speculative, but these developments seem highly likely given the current direction of sports, entertainment, and technology. Regardless of what the future holds, the ability to adapt to change, seize new opportunities, and navigate challenges will be crucial for athletes to maximize their NIL value in the years to come.

TEN

MAINTAINING A SUSTAINABLE NIL CAREER

While many athletes may initially focus on immediate opportunities to leverage their NIL rights, building a sustainable NIL career requires long-term strategic planning. The strategies discussed in this section aim to provide a roadmap for athletes seeking to maximize the value of their NIL rights throughout their entire careers.

CONTINUOUS PERSONAL BRAND DEVELOPMENT

Building a strong personal brand is vital for long-term NIL success. The brand you build defines who you are as an athlete and a person and forms the core of your value proposition to sponsors and fans. Continually refining and redefining your personal brand, and aligning it with your evolving personal values, experiences, and goals is essential. This includes staying true to your personality and values, maintaining a positive public image, and effectively promoting your brand through various channels, especially social media.

ESTABLISHING A DIVERSE REVENUE PORTFOLIO

Relying solely on one source of income can be risky, especially when it comes to NIL opportunities. Like any good investment strategy, diversification is key. This might include endorsement deals, sponsored content on social media, personal merchandise, revenue from streaming platforms, public speaking engagements, coaching opportunities, and more. A diverse revenue portfolio not only provides financial security but also allows you to explore different facets of your personal brand.

ENGAGING WITH FANS AND BUILDING A LOYAL FOLLOWING

Again, your fans are the backbone of your NIL value. Engaging with your fans, understanding their needs and interests, and building a strong relationship with them is crucial for long-term success. This can be done through social media interactions, fan events, personalized content, and more. The goal is to create a loyal fan base that will support you throughout your career, not just during your peak athletic performance years.

INVESTING IN CONTINUOUS LEARNING AND DEVELOPMENT

The world of NIL is dynamic and complex. To stay ahead, continuous learning and development are crucial. This includes staying informed about changes in legislation, market trends, and emerging opportunities. Additionally, learning about business principles, financial management, contract negotiation, and other related areas can enhance your ability to manage and grow your NIL career.

DEVELOPING A STRONG SUPPORT NETWORK

The importance of a solid support network cannot be overstated. This includes family, friends, mentors, agents, managers, and financial advisors. These individuals can provide guidance, emotional support, business advice, and industry connections that can help you navigate the challenges and opportunities of a NIL career.

MAINTAINING BALANCE AND PRIORITIZING HEALTH

Success in NIL, like in sports, requires balance. This includes balancing your athletic responsibilities, personal life, and NIL activities. Prioritizing your physical and mental health is crucial. Overworking and stress can lead to burnout, affecting your performance and overall well-being. It's important to create a routine that allows for adequate rest, nutrition, exercise, and personal time.

PLANNING FOR POST-ATHLETIC CAREER OPPORTUNITIES

Your NIL career doesn't have to end when your athletic career does. Planning for post-athletic career opportunities can help ensure a sustainable income flow. This might include roles in coaching, broadcasting, public speaking, brand ambassadorships, or other areas related to your sport or personal interests.

These strategies form a holistic approach to maintaining a sustainable NIL career. They aim to create a balance between immediate income generation and long-term success, between personal fulfillment and public appeal, and between risk and reward. It's a challenging path, but with strategic planning, diligence, and adaptability, it's a path that can lead to fulfilling and financially rewarding opportunities.

NAVIGATING INTELLECTUAL PROPERTY REGISTRATION

To safeguard your NIL rights, it's important to consider registering them as intellectual property. This process can feel daunting, but with a clear understanding and the right guidance, you can successfully navigate it. The following sections will outline the process of registering a copyright and a trademark with the United States Copyright Office and the United States Patent and Trademark Office, both of which are departments within the Library of Congress.

1. **Complete the Application**: Visit the United States Copyright Office website and click on "Register a Copyright." Fill out the online application form.

2. **Pay the Fee**: Pay the necessary filing fee.

3. **Wait for Processing**: After submitting your application, it will be processed, which can take several months.

Remember, a work is protected by copyright law as soon as it's created and fixed in a tangible form, even without registration. However, registering the copyright provides legal advantages, such as public record of ownership and the ability to sue for copyright infringement.

REGISTERING A TRADEMARK

A trademark protects words, phrases, symbols, or designs that distinguish the source of goods or services of one party from those of others. To register a trademark, follow these steps:

1. **Determine If a Trademark is Necessary**: If the mark distinguishes your goods or services and helps customers identify their source, it may be beneficial to register it.

2. **Check Trademark Database**: Before applying, search the United States Patent and Trademark Office's Trademark Electronic Search System (TESS) to ensure the mark is not already in use.

3. **File an Application**: You can file a trademark application online using the Trademark Electronic

Application System (TEAS), available on the United States Patent and Trademark Office website.

4. **Pay the Fee:** Pay the necessary filing fee, which varies depending on the type of application form.

5. **Monitor the Status:** After submitting, monitor the status of your application through the Trademark Status and Document Retrieval (TSDR) system.

6. **Respond to Office Actions or Notices:** If the trademark examining attorney sends any correspondence, respond in a timely manner to prevent abandonment of your application.

7. **Maintain Your Trademark:** Once registered, maintain your trademark by filing required maintenance documents and demonstrating continuous use in commerce.

Remember that the trademark registration process is nuanced and legal advice is often beneficial. Also, keep in mind that while registering provides the strongest protection, common law rights exist for unregistered trademarks based on the legitimate use of the mark.

DIVERSIFYING YOUR NIL PORTFOLIO

In an increasingly dynamic and uncertain world, diversification is a crucial strategy for managing risk and maximizing opportunities. For athletes, diversifying the NIL portfolio is about spreading your opportunities across different NIL revenue streams to ensure a stable income, especially as your athletic career evolves.

UNDERSTANDING YOUR UNIQUE VALUE PROPOSITION

Each athlete brings a unique value proposition to the NIL marketplace, shaped by factors like athletic accomplishments, personal characteristics, lifestyle, interests, and more. Understanding your unique value proposition can help identify potential opportunities for diversification that align with your personal brand.

EXPLORING DIVERSE NIL REVENUE STREAMS

There are various avenues an athlete can explore to diversify their NIL portfolio. As a quick recap, here are a few to consider:

1. **Sponsorships and Endorsements**: These are direct partnerships with companies that want to use your Name, Image, or Likeness to promote their products or services. They can take the form of cash payments, product giveaways, or equity in the company.

2. **Social Media and Content Creation**: Social media platforms and content creation outlets offer a wide range of opportunities for athletes to earn income, engage with fans, and promote their personal brand. These might include sponsored posts, ad revenue, crowdfunding, subscriptions, merchandise sales, and more.

3. **Public Speaking and Appearances**: Athletes can leverage their fame and personal stories to generate income through public speaking

engagements, appearances at events, autograph signings, and more.

4. **Coaching and Training**: Athletes can monetize their expertise and skills by offering coaching, training, or consulting services.

5. **Investments and Equity Deals**: Athletes can invest in businesses, real estate, stocks, or other assets to generate income. Some endorsement deals also offer equity stakes, giving athletes a share in the company's future success.

BALANCING RISK AND REWARD

While diversification can help manage risk, it's important to balance the potential rewards against the time and energy required for each opportunity. Some revenue streams might offer high-income potential but require significant time and effort. Others might offer lower income but align more closely with your personal interests and brand.

CASE STUDIES: ATHLETES WITH SUSTAINABLE NIL CAREERS

Analyzing case studies of athletes who've successfully sustained their NIL careers can provide valuable insights and lessons. Here are a few examples:

Case Study 1: LeBron James

NBA superstar LeBron James has successfully diversified his NIL portfolio, investing in a range of businesses, including Blaze Pizza, and partnering with companies like Nike, Sprite, and Beats by Dre. He's also expanded into entertainment, co-founding the production company SpringHill Entertainment.

Case Study 2: Serena Williams

Tennis legend Serena Williams has not only been successful on the court but also off it. She's used her fame and influence to build a business empire that includes the clothing line S by Serena, venture capital firm Serena Ventures, and partnerships with companies like Nike and Gatorade.

Case Study 3: Tom Brady

NFL star Tom Brady has monetized his NIL through endorsement deals with companies like Under Armour and UGG, co-founding the health and wellness company TB12, and launching the NFT platform Autograph.

Case Study 4: Alex Morgan

US soccer player Alex Morgan has diversified her NIL portfolio with endorsement deals with companies like Nike, Coca-Cola, and McDonald's, co-authoring a series of children's books, and investing in the professional women's soccer team Angel City FC.

Case Study 5: Cristiano Ronaldo

Known as one of the greatest footballers of all time, Cristiano Ronaldo has made his mark off the field as well. His lucrative endorsement deals include brands such as Nike, Herbalife, and KFC. He also has his own clothing line, CR7, which includes everything from shoes to perfumes.

Case Study 6: Naomi Osaka

A tennis superstar, Naomi Osaka has quickly become a major player in the NIL space, signing deals with Nike, Yonex, and Nissan, among others. Osaka also invested in the North Carolina Courage of the National Women's Soccer League and launched her own skincare line, KINLÒ, designed specifically for people with melanated skin.

Case Study 7: Stephen Curry

NBA superstar Stephen Curry has cultivated a diverse NIL portfolio, which includes endorsements with Under Armour, Chase, and Rakuten. He's also the co-founder of Unanimous Media, a production company, and SC30 Inc., a company that manages his brand partnerships and philanthropic ventures.

Case Study 8: Maria Sharapova

Retired tennis professional Maria Sharapova has success-fully sustained her NIL career post-retirement. She founded the premium candy line Sugarpova and secured partner-ships with Porsche, Evian, and TAG Heuer. Additionally, Sharapova is a strategic investor and an ambassador for the tech wellness company, Therabody.

Case Study 9: Michael Phelps

The most decorated Olympian of all time, Michael Phelps, leveraged his NIL through partnerships with Under Armour, Omega, and Subway, and by launching his competitive swimwear brand, MP. Post-retirement, Phelps continues to be involved in various mental health initiatives, further solidifying his legacy both in and out of the pool.

Case Study 10: Simone Biles

Known as the greatest gymnast ever, Simone Biles has built a successful NIL career through partnerships with major brands like Nike, Kellogg's, and Hershey's. She's also a co-owner of the gymnastics training center, World Champions Centre, and an advocate for mental health and body positivity.

These athletes have all capitalized on their NIL rights in dif-ferent ways, reflecting their unique personal brands, inter-ests, and values. Their success underscores the importance of diversification, strategic planning, and adaptability in maintaining a sustainable NIL career.

PLANNING FOR A LONG-TERM NIL CAREER

When it comes to maintaining a long-term NIL career, sound financial management and planning are critical. Unlike traditional nine-to-five jobs, an athlete's income can be significantly variable and uncertain. This chapter provides a comprehensive guide to financial planning and management strategies to secure your NIL income and ensure its longevity.

UNDERSTANDING YOUR FINANCIAL LANDSCAPE

The first step to effective financial management is understanding your financial landscape. This includes income sources from NIL deals, expenses, taxes, and other financial obligations. You should also consider the lifespan of your current contracts, your career longevity, and potential future income.

BUDGETING AND EXPENSE MANAGEMENT

As we discussed in the previous chapter, a detailed and realistic budget is a powerful tool for managing your finances. It should account for all your income and expenditures, including living expenses, taxes, training costs, travel, insurance, and lifestyle expenses.

Expense management is equally crucial. With sudden wealth often comes the temptation to make lavish purchases. While it's reasonable to enjoy your hard-earned money, it's vital to avoid frivolous spending that can quickly erode your wealth.

INVESTING FOR THE FUTURE

Investing is a powerful tool for growing and preserving wealth over the long term. Instead of keeping all your money in a savings account, consider investing in a diversified portfolio of assets. These might include stocks, bonds, real estate, or even businesses.

RETIREMENT PLANNING

Even at the peak of your athletic career, it's essential to start planning for retirement. This might involve contributing to a retirement account, investing in an annuity, or building a portfolio of income-generating assets.

WORKING WITH PROFESSIONALS

To navigate these complex financial issues, consider working with professionals like financial advisors, accountants, and lawyers. They can provide valuable advice, manage your finances, ensure tax compliance, and protect your legal interests.

HEALTH MANAGEMENT: BALANCING ATHLETIC DEMANDS FOR SUSTAINABLE NIL SUCCESS

As we discussed briefly in Chapter Eight, maintaining peak physical condition is crucial for athletes. However, the physical demands of sports can put athletes at risk of injuries, which can significantly impact their NIL value. This section explores strategies for managing health to sustain your NIL success.

UNDERSTANDING THE HEALTH RISKS

Different sports carry different health risks. Understanding these risks can help you make informed decisions about your training, competition schedules, and health management strategies. As a quick recap, here's what you need to remember:

- **Prevention and Early Intervention**: Prevention is the best medicine. Regular check-ups, a balanced diet, adequate rest, proper equipment, and a good understanding of your sport can prevent injuries and health problems.

- **Rehabilitation and Recovery**: In case of injuries, proper rehabilitation and recovery are essential to regain your athletic performance and preserve your NIL value. This might involve physical therapy, surgeries, rest, or modifications to your training regimen.

- **Mental Health**: Mental health is just as important as physical health. The pressure to perform and the scrutiny that comes with fame can take a toll on mental health. Regular check-ups with a psychologist, mindfulness practices, and a strong support network can help maintain mental well-being.

- **Health Insurance**: Health insurance is a crucial risk management tool that can cover the cost of medical treatments, rehabilitation, and other health-related expenses. It's important to understand your insurance coverage, including what's covered, the cost of premiums, and the process for making a claim.

- **Work-Life Balance**: Maintaining a work-life balance can help manage stress, prevent burnout, and sustain your athletic performance and NIL career over the long term. This might involve scheduling rest periods, pursuing hobbies, spending time with loved ones, or engaging in other non-sport activities.

By carefully managing your finances and health, you can maximize your NIL earnings, preserve your athletic performance, and sustain a long and successful NIL career.

LOOKING AHEAD: THE FUTURE OF SUSTAINABLE NIL CAREERS

In the dynamic world of sports, uncertainty is the only constant. Changes in regulations, evolving market trends, and even personal athletic performance can significantly impact an athlete's NIL career. Therefore, it's essential to look ahead and consider the future landscape of NIL careers and strategies to ensure sustainability.

PREDICTED CHANGES IN THE NIL LANDSCAPE

Just as the NIL legislation transformed the college sports industry, future regulatory changes could have far-reaching implications for athletes and their NIL earnings. Potential changes might include further loosening of restrictions, allowing for even more lucrative opportunities. Conversely, increased regulation could limit NIL earnings or introduce additional legal and compliance burdens.

Technological advances are also expected to shape the future of NIL careers. For example, the rise of social media and online platforms has created numerous new opportunities for athletes to monetize their NIL. Continued technological innovation could lead to even more platforms and formats for NIL monetization, such as virtual reality or augmented reality experiences.

Moreover, evolving societal trends will impact the NIL landscape. For instance, growing awareness about mental health, diversity, and social issues could create opportunities for athletes who champion these causes. At the same time, public expectations and scrutiny could increase, requiring athletes to carefully manage their public image and actions.

STRATEGIES FOR SUSTAINABLE NIL CAREERS

Given these predicted changes, athletes will need to adopt proactive strategies to sustain their NIL careers.

1. **Adaptability**: Adaptability will be crucial in navigating future changes. This might involve adjusting to new regulations, learning new technologies, or rebranding to align with societal trends. Athletes should remain open to new opportunities and be willing to pivot as the landscape evolves.

2. **Continuous Learning and Development**: As the NIL landscape becomes more complex, athletes will

need to constantly update their knowledge and skills. This might involve understanding new legislation, mastering new technologies, or learning about finance, marketing, and branding. Athletes might consider working with mentors, taking courses, or attending industry events to stay informed.

3. **Personal Branding**: As societal trends and public expectations evolve, personal branding will become increasingly important. Athletes will need to cultivate a positive and authentic personal brand that resonates with fans, sponsors, and the public. This might involve championing social causes, sharing personal stories, or demonstrating values like integrity, resilience, and commitment.

4. **Risk Management**: Risk management will be even more critical in the future NIL landscape. This might involve diversifying NIL income sources, investing wisely, securing comprehensive insurance coverage, and maintaining physical and mental health. It also means having crisis management plans in case of injuries, scandals, or sudden loss of income.

5. **Relationship Building**: Building strong relationships will be key to long-term NIL success.

This includes relationships with fans, sponsors, agents, financial advisors, and even other athletes. A strong network can provide support, advice, and opportunities, helping athletes navigate challenges and seize new opportunities.

As the NIL landscape continues to evolve, so too will the strategies for sustaining a long-term NIL career. By looking ahead and proactively preparing for these changes, athletes can ensure they're well-positioned to adapt, thrive, and sustain their NIL success into the future.

—— CONCLUSION ——

THE FUTURE OF NIL

A s we reach the end of this exploration of Name, Image, and Likeness, it's fitting to cast our gaze toward the horizon and consider the exciting and uncertain future of NIL. It is clear that the landscape of NIL is evolving at a rapid pace, driven by the relentless march of technological innovation and changing societal norms. As we stand on the cusp of this brave new world, it's crucial to understand and embrace the changes and challenges that lie ahead.

UPCOMING TRENDS AND THEIR IMPACT ON NIL

Several emerging trends promise to reshape the world of NIL in the coming years. The rise of the metaverse, the proliferation of AI and machine learning, and the increasing use of blockchain technology and NFTs, all present incredible opportunities for athletes to leverage and monetize their NIL in new and innovative ways.

BLOCKCHAIN AND NFTS

Blockchain technology and NFTs are set to revolutionize the sports industry, providing new opportunities for athletes to monetize their NIL. NFTs are unique digital assets stored on a blockchain, and they can represent ownership of anything from a piece of artwork to a moment in a sports game.

For athletes, NFTs can offer a unique and innovative way to monetize their NIL. For example, an athlete could create an NFT of a highlight from their career and auction it off to fans. Or, they could release a series of NFT trading cards featuring their image and likeness. Given the unique nature of NFTs and their potential for high value, this could become a significant source of NIL income for athletes.

VIRTUAL AND AUGMENTED REALITY

VR and AR are also expected to shape the future of NIL. These technologies can create immersive experiences, allowing fans to feel closer to their favorite athletes than ever before.

For instance, a VR experience could allow a fan to virtually attend a training session with their favorite athlete, while an AR app could let fans take selfies with an augmented version of the athlete. These technologies provide new and exciting ways for athletes to engage with fans, potentially leading to increased NIL opportunities.

ARTIFICIAL INTELLIGENCE (AI)

AI has the potential to be a game-changer for NIL. AI-powered analytics could provide deeper insights into fan engagement and behaviors, helping athletes optimize their NIL strategies. Furthermore, AI could be used to create personalized fan experiences, such as AI-powered chatbots in the athlete's persona, increasing engagement and creating new NIL opportunities.

As we move forward, it's clear that the world of NIL will continue to evolve, bringing new opportunities and challenges for athletes. By staying informed about these trends and technologies and adapting their strategies accordingly, athletes can ensure they're well-positioned to maximize their NIL value in the future.

CONTINUED IMPACT OF SOCIAL MEDIA

Irrespective, it is important to still remember that the influence of social media on NIL will only increase in the future. Platforms like TikTok, Instagram, and X (formerly Twitter) allow athletes to interact with their fans directly, making these platforms ripe for NIL opportunities. As we've seen in recent years, the more followers an athlete has, the more attractive they become to brands.

In the future, new social media platforms and features are expected to emerge, offering even more opportunities for athletes to monetize their NIL. We can also expect to see more sophistication in how social media data is used, with advanced analytics helping athletes understand which content resonates most with their audience, allowing them to maximize their engagement and, by extension, their NIL value.

THE RISE OF E-SPORTS AND VIRTUAL ATHLETES

The rapid growth of e-sports and virtual gaming has presented a new frontier for NIL. As these platforms continue to gain popularity, athletes who establish a presence in the gaming world can tap into a whole new fan base.

Moreover, the concept of "virtual athletes"—characters in video games, simulations, or virtual worlds—offers an intriguing possibility. These virtual personas can be designed, marketed, and monetized, much like their real-world counterparts, potentially opening up new avenues for NIL income.

FINAL THOUGHTS

The NIL landscape is dynamic, with new opportunities and challenges constantly emerging. In this ever-changing environment, it's crucial for athletes to remain adaptable and forward-thinking. They must be willing to embrace new technologies, diversify their NIL portfolios, and continuously learn and adapt to the evolving rules and regulations surrounding NIL.

The journey to unlocking the full power of NIL is an ongoing one, but with careful planning, strategic decision-making, and a willingness to innovate, athletes can not only navigate this complex landscape but thrive within it.

As the world of NIL continues to evolve, we'll likely see more changes on the horizon. But one thing is for sure: the power of NIL offers exciting opportunities for athletes to monetize their fame, and these opportunities will only expand in the years to come. As we move into this new era, athletes who can successfully manage their NIL will have a significant advantage, both during their athletic careers and long after they've left the playing field.

Amidst all the excitement and potential of NIL, it's vital not to lose sight of the values that underpin sport: passion, integrity, and the pursuit of excellence. After all, it is these values that make sport such a powerful platform for personal brand building and NIL monetization.

It is our hope that this book has provided you with the insights and tools you need to unlock the power of NIL and navigate this exciting new landscape with confidence and success. As you embark on your NIL journey, we wish you the very best of luck, and we look forward to seeing you shine.

ACKNOWLEDGMENTS

We are immensely grateful to a number of people whose guidance, support, and inspiration have been pivotal in the realization of this book.

First, we must express our profound gratitude to our families. Thank you for your unwavering faith in us and for your boundless love that enriches our lives. To our friends, thank you for your encouragement and for always believing in us, even when the path seemed uncertain.

We extend our sincere thanks to our colleagues and mentors who have shared their insights and expertise. Your wisdom and encouragement have been indispensable. We are also grateful to the team of editors, designers, and publishers whose hard work and dedication have brought the pages of this book to life.

A special thank you to Shayne Beecher, Phil Petrina, and Ryan Joline who were co-contributors to this project. Their insight and wisdom have proven invaluable, significantly enriching this message.

Thank you to my parents, who have always believed in me. Thank you to God. He makes all things possible. Thank you to every one of you who are traversing this journey with us. Together we will change the world of student athletics forever.—Ryan Joline

A special thank you goes to the University of Pittsburgh for embracing this project as part of their curriculum and to all the aspiring student-athletes who inspire us daily with their passion and dedication to their crafts.

Lastly, we are thankful to the readers and supporters of this work. Your engagement and feedback make all the efforts worthwhile.

Thank you all for being part of this journey.

ABOUT THE AUTHOR

Jason Grilli is a former professional athlete and a passionate advocate for athlete empowerment. With profound insight in Name, Image, and Likeness policies, Jason has become a highly sought-after advisor for young athletes. He was a 2013 National League All-Star and played for eight different MLB teams, including the Pittsburgh Pirates and Toronto Blue Jays. Jason uses his platform to support the next generation of athletes, emphasizing the importance of navigating complexities with integrity.

This information is constantly evolving and changing. For the most ever green content, please scan the QR code to access our website.

www.ingramcontent.com/pod-product-compliance
Lightning Source LLC
Chambersburg PA
CBHW071551210326
41597CB00019B/3197